THY
KINGDOM
COME

TONY EVANS

THY KINGDOM COME

EXPLORING END TIMES PROPHECY

MOODY PUBLISHERS

CHICAGO

This book is excerpted and condensed from chapters 1–15 of *The Best Is Yet to Come: Bible Prophecies Through the Ages*, © 2000 by Anthony T. Evans (Moody Publishers).

Scripture quotations taken from the (NASB®) New American Standard Bible®, Copyright © 1960, 1971, 1977, 1995 by The Lockman Foundation. Used by permission. All rights reserved. lockman.org

Edited by Kevin Mungons
Interior design: Ragont Design
Cover design: Thinkpen Design
Cover photo of St. Peter's Basilica courtesy of Unsplash, Chad Greiter
Author photo: Tayte Rian Gerik

ISBN: 978–0–8024–3313–8

Originally delivered by fleets of horse-drawn wagons, the affordable paperbacks from D. L. Moody's publishing house resourced the church and served everyday people. Now, after more than 125 years of publishing and ministry, Moody Publishers' mission remains the same—even if our delivery systems have changed a bit. For more information on other books (and resources) created from a biblical perspective, go to www.moodypublishers.com or write to:

Moody Publishers
820 N. LaSalle Boulevard
Chicago, IL 60610

1 3 5 7 9 10 8 6 4 2

Printed in the United States of America

CONTENTS

INTRODUCTION

The global events which seem to be unfolding and developing anew each day inspire within each of us a greater understanding and awareness of biblical prophecy. Yet anyone who has attempted to teach this subject of prophecy knows it is no easy task. To seek to thread together the prophetic strands of Scripture in an orderly and relevant way is, without question, one of the most difficult things I have ever faced as a preacher and Bible scholar. It has required intense study, research, and prayer.

In the pages that follow, I humbly attempt to unveil insights on this popular and far too relevant area of prophecy. I seek to communicate the prophetic program of God in a logical and easy-to-understand way. My desire in doing so is not simply to stimulate your mind but also to influence your heart. I want to cause you to fall more deeply in love with the God who holds eternity in His hands.

Studying prophecy is like traveling in space. We've learned a lot about the earth by going out into space and looking back at our planet. Through scientific study we have learned about weather patterns, the location of natural resources, and other beneficial things that we might not have known about if we had stayed close to the earth.

In the same way, prophecy takes us beyond the limitations of our time-and-space-bound world and circumstances and lets us see the big picture. The result should be that we become better stewards of our time and other resources now as we live in light of eternity. It is my hope and prayer that after you have seen and understood God's plan for the ages, you will love Him more and serve Him more fully as His kingdom disciple.

PART ONE

The History of Fulfilled Prophecy

1

THE IMPORTANCE OF PROPHECY

When you go to a movie theater, the first twenty minutes will be spent viewing previews of upcoming attractions. These include the hot clips of what's to come. At the end of each preview, you will often see the month or the year that the new show will air. Sometimes, though, you will only see "coming soon."

Studying prophecy can be a lot like previews of upcoming attractions. We aren't given the whole show, but we do get glimpses into the highlights. Sometimes prophecy gives an exact date, like in the case of Daniel's dream interpretation, but most of the time it just says, "Coming soon." One thing that is always consistent is that prophecy involves the study of the future. It lifts our thoughts from the midst of the ticking clock of time and allows us to peek into the future.

Tomorrow is as real to God as today or yesterday because God is an eternal Being. God is not bound by time like we are. In fact, time designations have no meaning to Him. That's why God identified Himself to Moses as the great "I AM" (Ex. 3:14). He is forever in the present tense, the now.

But because the eternal God has chosen to unfurl His plan for creation in time, prophecy—the study of future things—is very important.

Most of us have a natural desire to know the future, to try to find out what tomorrow will bring. That's why so many people turn to psychics or horoscopes. The people who sell you supposed knowledge of the future are preying on people's desire to put together the jigsaw puzzle of life, whether it's the collective history of a nation or an individual life. People want to know how things are going to unfold.

I don't know about anyone else, but if I want to know something about what the future holds, I want to get my information from a reliable source. I don't want to stake my life on what some horoscope might say.

The main problem with these so-called psychic "prophets" of the future is that they are *false* prophets. They are feeding people lies because they don't truly know about the future, either on an individual or cosmic level. They are guessing. Even worse, sometimes they are demonically inspired. Bible prophecy is not designed to satisfy our curiosity about tomorrow or the next day, nor is it designed to fill our heads with information so we can get together and debate the details of God's plan. Gaining information has its place in the study of prophecy. It's important that we understand as fully as we can what God is saying to us. But at the heart of God's purpose for prophecy is changing our hearts and affecting the way we live our lives.

As we start our study of the wonderful and complex revelation of God concerning prophecy, I want to help you see how important prophecy is. The last chapter of the Bible says:

> I testify to everyone who hears the words of the prophecy of this book: if anyone adds to them, God shall add to him the plagues which are written in this book; and if anyone takes away from the words of the book of this prophecy, God shall take away his part from the tree of life and from the holy city, which are written in this book. (Rev. 22:18–19)

Prophecy is very serious business with God. Mess with His prophetic Word, and it will mess you up as well. God's prophetic message is so important that He announced a curse on anyone who tampers with it.

Let me say right up front that I know everybody does not agree on every interpretation of God's prophetic program. There are various views within the Christian community about exactly when Jesus will come back and the shape His kingdom will take. But these varieties of interpretations, if they remain within the sphere of orthodoxy, do not have to hamper us from gaining a broad understanding of what God has in store for His people.

So let's get started on this fascinating, awe-inspiring subject by considering the importance of prophecy. In this chapter, I want to answer the questions:

What makes this study significant to your life right now, where you are? and,

Why should you and I be vitally concerned about God's prophetic agenda?

PROPHECY HELPS AUTHENTICATE THE BIBLE

People often ask how we Christians can claim that the Bible is true as opposed to any other holy book. What makes the Bible distinct from other writings that claim to be from God?

The Bible's Prophetic Accuracy

There are many answers to that question, but one thing that sets the Bible apart is its prophetic accuracy. A large portion of biblical prophecy has already been fulfilled with flawless exactness. Events that one author wrote about were fulfilled precisely hundreds of years later.

One of the classic examples is the prophecy of Jesus' birth in Bethlehem by the prophet Micah more than seven hundred years before the event (Mic. 5:2; cf. Matt. 2:1–6). If Bethlehem had been a major metropolis in Israel, someone could argue it was a good guess. But Micah pinpointed an obscure village because he spoke the mind of God. The fulfillment of prophecies like this helps to validate the truth of the Bible.

Of course, Micah's prophecy is just one of several hundred biblical prophecies that were fulfilled in Christ's first coming alone. This validation of the Bible by prophecy is a strong argument to believe the many prophecies that are yet to be fulfilled.

The Divine Origin of Prophecy

In 2 Peter 1:20–21, the apostle wrote, "Know this first of all, that no prophecy of Scripture is a matter of one's own interpretation, for no prophecy was ever made by an act of human will, but men moved by the Holy Spirit spoke from God." The accuracy of the Bible's predictions should not surprise us, because this was not human writers doing guesswork. Prophetic Scripture is accurate in all of its details because God moved the authors to record what was said.

Someone who was good with numbers and probabilities figured out that it would require 100 billion earths populated with 8 billion people each to come up with one person who could achieve 100 prophecies accurately without any errors in sequence. In other words, it would be impossible. But the Bible contains hundreds of prophecies that have already come true. That's because it's not based on chance, but on the eternal knowledge of God.

PROPHECY REVEALS GOD'S CHARACTER

The second reason prophecy is important is that it reveals to us the character of God. When you understand God's program, you get to know more about Him.

In Isaiah 46, the prophet made a powerful statement about God's character and knowledge as it relates to His prophetic program:

Remember this, and be assured;
Recall it to mind, you transgressors.
Remember the former things long past,
for I am God, and there is no other;
I am God, and there is no one like Me,
Declaring the end from the beginning,
And from ancient times things which have not been done,
Saying, 'My purpose will be established,
And I will accomplish all My good pleasure'; . . .
I have planned it, surely I will do it. (vv. 8–10, 11c)

Whatever God plans, He accomplishes. No part of His will can ever be outwitted or thwarted by the mind of man. God was not caught off guard by human sin, because His plan for this universe was drawn up and nailed down in eternity past. But this raises a question for a lot of people. If God planned everything and nothing can change His plan, why should we do anything? Why not just sit back and take it easy, because what's going to happen is going to happen anyway?

The answer is that God's sovereignty does not relieve us of our human responsibility. We are still obligated to live righteously, because God is holy and just and cannot tolerate sin. And God will use our obedience to help accomplish His plan.

I realize there is plenty of mystery here because God's knowledge of the future includes not only everything that actually happens, but everything that could potentially happen. God knows all possibilities in any circumstance, but He chooses what *will* happen according to His will and purpose.

The word *surprise* is not in God's vocabulary. He never says, "Oops, I missed that one." All possibilities are taken into consideration. God's plan takes in "the end from the beginning." There are no surprises in heaven—absolutely none!

Prophecy not only reveals the character of God in terms of His perfect knowledge and power, but also in terms of His purpose to bring Himself glory and bless His people. Paul said of his trials, "I consider that the sufferings of this present time are not worthy to be compared with the glory that is to be revealed to us" (Rom. 8:18). The apostle knew that the suffering God was allowing in his life would work out to God's greater glory and his greater reward. Paul could say this because he believed Christ's message about a future hope that was laid up for Paul, and "not only to [him], but also to all who have loved His appearing" (2 Tim. 4:8).

A knowledge of prophecy gives you confidence to trust God for what's ahead. If God knows tomorrow already because He has been there and taken care of it, then you can go to sleep tonight confident that He is in control.

Prophecy enhances our understanding of the character of God and leads us to worship Him. Over and over again in his letters, Paul became so overwhelmed with God's character that he couldn't help but worship when he considered God's powerful plan.

PROPHECY PROMOTES HOLINESS

A third reason for studying prophecy is that it is designed to promote holy living. The more conscious we are of Christ's return, and of the fact that we could be standing face-to-face with Him at any moment, the more this knowledge will affect us. But if we forget that Jesus is coming back, we will start living like He's not coming back. John gave a classic statement of prophecy's purifying purpose. "We know that when He appears, we shall be like Him, because we will see Him just as He is. And everyone who has this hope fixed on Him purifies himself, just as He is pure" (1 John 3:2–3).

A Prize to Be Won

Let's look at this issue in more detail since it is so crucial. Paul said, "I press on toward the goal for the prize of the upward call of God in Christ Jesus" (Phil. 3:14). Paul was determined to remain faithful to Christ because there was a heavenly prize to be won when Christ returned.

God's prophetic program included a reward for Paul, one that was worth all of his commitment on earth. And he urged all believers to adopt the same attitude (v. 15). There's a lot we will do if there's a big enough prize at the end of the process. Paul went on to explain his perspective: "Our citizenship is in heaven, from which also we eagerly wait for a Savior, the Lord Jesus Christ; who will transform the body of our humble state into conformity with the body of His glory" (vv. 20–21).

Paul said, "I'm really a citizen of heaven. I just have a temporary address here on earth." Because Paul had such a high consciousness of eternity, he pressed on in history.

You can keep going, no matter what, when you know heaven is real. You can keep going if you understand that when your human body begins to decay on earth, you have just begun to live forever.

A Hope to Be Realized

John said our hope of Christ's return should purify us. Paul agreed, writing in Titus 2:

For the grace of God has appeared, bringing salvation to all men, instructing us to deny ungodliness and worldly desires and to live sensibly, righteously and godly in the present age, looking for the blessed hope and the appearing of the glory of our great God and Savior, Christ Jesus. (vv. 11–13)

Notice the three distinct perspectives Paul mentioned here. Christians are people who are looking in three directions. We look back at the cross and remember what Christ has done. We look inwardly to see what Christ is doing in us today. And we look forward to the day when Christ will return for us.

A Perspective to Gain

Peter also had something to say about the way prophecy ought to promote holy living:

> The day of the Lord will come like a thief, in which the heavens will pass away with a roar and the elements will be destroyed with intense heat, and the earth and its works will be burned up.
>
> Since all these things are to be destroyed in this way, what sort of people ought you to be in holy conduct and godliness, looking for and hastening the coming of the day of God. (2 Peter 3:10–12a)

Peter said a day is coming when your house, your car, the clothes in your closet, and the money in your bank will burn. The earth as we know it is going to melt away. Since that's true, don't start treating that stuff as if it were eternal. Don't fall so deeply in love with the stuff that's going to burn that you miss out on the stuff that can't burn. Don't trade the things that have eternal value for the things that won't make it to heaven.

It's okay to have a house and car and clothes. Just don't put a value on them they don't have. Don't treat them like they're the real deal because when Jesus returns, they are going to be toast. It's okay to use the world, but not to be dominated by a worldly perspective (see 1 Cor. 7:31). Rather, we should all live with a kingdom worldview based on God's kingdom values.

A good understanding of prophecy can give us a reference point for living. When a farmer wants to plow a straight furrow, he picks out a marker at the other side of the field and keeps his eyes on it as he plows. You need a reference point when you're looking into the future. If you're just entering college and you want to be a doctor, that's your reference point. Your goal will determine what courses you take and the path you follow. You will most certainly set your sights on medical school.

The Bible says if you fix your sights and your hope on Christ's coming, that perspective on tomorrow will influence your thoughts and choices today. Prophecy can help you stay on God's kingdom path so that you can produce fruit for eternity.

A Future to Prepare For

Paul also said he lived in light of one inescapable fact. Speaking of the judgment of believers for kingdom reward, or the lack thereof, he wrote, "We must all appear before the judgment seat of Christ, so that each one may be recompensed for his deeds in the body" (2 Cor. 5:10).

This is how I picture the judgment seat of Christ taking place. Most stores today have security cameras recording a customer's every move. Some stores even alert people to that fact as they enter the store.

When I first saw those signs, I wondered why the stores were advertising the fact that they used security cameras. After all, the idea is to catch a thief in the act. But as I thought about it, the reason for the warning signs became clear. People who know someone is watching their every move will probably think twice before trying anything funny. But if they don't think anyone is watching, they'll be more likely to take a chance and steal something.

Well, our lives are being watched and recorded by God. At Christ's judgment seat, He will sit down with us to view our lives. When you have a prophetic mindset, it will affect your preparation for eternity. Prophecy can help give us a prepared mindset. It's important because it promotes holy living on the part of believers.

PROPHECY BRINGS STABILITY IN TRIALS

Stability in times of difficulty is a fourth reason prophecy is important to us. Knowing what tomorrow holds for us can help us be strong in the storms of today.

A Calm in the Storm

In the upper room, as He celebrated the Last Supper with His disciples, Jesus told them He was about to leave them. Their response was, "How are we going to make it?"

To reassure His faithful followers, Jesus spoke these well-known words of comfort:

> Do not let your heart be troubled; believe in God, believe also in Me. In My Father's house are many dwelling places; if it were not so, I would have told you; for I go to prepare a place for you. If I go and prepare a place for you, I will come again and receive you to Myself, that where I am, there you may be also. (John 14:1–3)

Jesus' prophecy of His own return helped produce calm in the midst of the disciples' panic.

Good News in Grief

One of the best examples of the use of prophecy to calm troubled hearts is in 1 Thessalonians 4:13–18, another familiar passage in which Paul comforted the Thessalonians concerning their fellow Christians who had died.

Verses 13–17 are Paul's teaching on the rapture, the moment when Christ will return in the air to take His people home to be with Him forever. This is one of the great, central passages of prophecy in the

Bible. Yet Paul wasn't just dispensing doctrine. He closed this section by saying, "Therefore comfort one another with these words" (v. 18).

Hope for the Future

We've mentioned this benefit of studying prophecy, but let me come back to it. The prophetic Word of God also brings us encouragement and hope for the future.

The Thessalonian church was shaken by the death of some of its members, because the believers weren't sure what had happened to these brothers and sisters. The church was also shaken by a false word from someone that the day of the Lord had already come. Paul answered that charge and put their fears at ease:

> Now we request you, brethren, with regard to the coming of our Lord Jesus Christ and our gathering together to Him, that you not be quickly shaken from your composure or be disturbed either by a spirit or a message or a letter as if from us, to the effect that the day of the Lord has come. (2 Thess. 2:1–2)

Paul proceeded to give them details by which the day of the Lord can be recognized, and we'll cover these in a subsequent chapter. What I want you to see here is the way Paul used this teaching to restore their hope. He concluded in verse 15, "So then, brethren, stand firm and hold to the traditions which you were taught, whether by word of mouth or by letter from us."

God wants to teach us about prophecy so we will stand firm today and not be thrown off by Satan or false teachers. If you're not alert, people will throw you off. The devil will throw you off. They can make your knees wobble. But if you know God's Word, you have a firm hope to hold on to even in the changing wind of circumstances.

A Right View of Life

In 2 Corinthians 5:8, Paul said, "We . . . prefer rather to be absent from the body and to be at home with the Lord." If you prefer heaven, you'll make it on earth. But if you prefer earth, you'll have a misperception of heaven. In other words, be heavenly. Colossians 3:2 says, "Set your mind on the things above, not on the things that are on earth." Your life should have such a heavenly dynamism about it that earth shrinks in significance.

The reason some of us aren't making it here on earth is because this life is too big. We've made the world too big, Satan too big, and people too big. They are ruining our day.

There's a lot to worry about today from a human standpoint. But if you have a firm grip on the fact that God has a prophetic program that nothing on earth can override, then you don't have to have a heart attack worrying about what might happen. Prophecy contributes to a right view of life.

PROPHECY PROMOTES WITNESSING

God does not tell us about the future so we can argue about it or show how much we know. He wants us to know the truth about tomorrow and about eternity, because people on their way to hell need to know God *today* before it's too late for them.

Let me show you several verses that underscore what I'm talking about. "It is a terrifying thing to fall into the hands of the living God" (Heb. 10:31). "Our God is a consuming fire" (Heb. 12:29). "Therefore, knowing the fear of the Lord, we persuade men" (2 Cor. 5:11). We are going to study a lot of prophecy in this book. Let's make sure we are telling others the good news of God's plan. Above all else, understanding prophecy should motivate us to witness to a world in need of Jesus Christ.

2

THE KEY TO PROPHECY

A key is important because it gives you access. A key that will unlock Bible prophecy, helping you see the individual details in their proper relationship and keep them in proper perspective, is hanging at the "door" of Revelation 19:10. After another awe-inspiring revelation by an angel, John was about to fall at the angel's feet in worship. But the angel told John, "Do not do that; I am a fellow servant of yours and your brethren who hold the testimony of Jesus; worship God. For the testimony of Jesus is the spirit of prophecy."

That's a profoundly important statement. It tells us that the key that unlocks the door to prophecy is not a thing or an idea, but a person. Jesus Christ is the key to God's prophetic revelation.

By this I mean that the degree to which prophetic details are related properly to Christ is the degree to which we will understand prophecy. God did not simply string together a series of prophetic events that happen one after another. There's a point, a definite climax, to God's plan. Prophecy, like history, is taking us somewhere.

And that destination is Jesus Christ. So if we study all the details and yet miss Christ, we have missed the point of prophecy.

You can see this in the people talking about prophecy and end times who aren't Christians. They can make their predictions and their guesses, but they have no Christ-centered reference point; they can't make sense out of things. Without Christ at the center of prophecy, that will always be true, because "the testimony of Jesus is the spirit of prophecy."

JESUS CHRIST IS THE CENTERPIECE OF PROPHECY

I want to look at four truths that are crucial to understand about the preeminent place Jesus Christ holds in the study of prophecy. Before we get to the plan, we need to see the person around whom God's plan unfolds.

The first thing we need to understand is that Jesus is the centerpiece of biblical prophecy.

Paul began the book of Titus by saying, "Paul, a bond-servant of God and an apostle of Jesus Christ, for the faith of those chosen of God and the knowledge of the truth which is according to godliness, in the hope of eternal life, which God, who cannot lie, promised long ages ago" (Titus 1:1–2).

The Recipient of God's Promise

The phrase "long ages ago" refers to eternity. Long before He created the world, God promised eternal life to those who would be chosen by Him. But to whom did God make this promise? It wasn't to you and me because we didn't yet exist. God the Father made this promise to His Son, the Lord Jesus. In 2 Timothy 1:9, Paul said the grace that saves us "was granted us in Christ Jesus from all eternity." In other words, we as believers were promised or given to Christ by His Father in eternity past.

Jesus Himself confirmed this when He said, "All that the Father gives Me shall come to Me, and the one who comes to Me I will certainly not cast out" (John 6:37). The Word could not be clearer. Every Christian is a gift from God the Father to God the Son.

The reason God the Father made this gift to His Son is that there exists such an intense love relationship among the members of the Trinity that They seek ways to express Their love. Jesus said, "The Father loves the Son" (John 5:20). One of the ways to express love is through a gift. God the Father has given the Son He loves a gift, a body of people who have put their faith in the Son. My point here is that Jesus is the delight of His Father, whose program centers on the Son.

The Goal of God's Gift

The Father's goal in giving Jesus Christ this gift is that we might become conformed to Christ's image (see Rom. 8:29). God's prophetic goal, if you will, is to create a group of people who look like Jesus. The Father does this, once again, because He loves His Son with infinite love. God wants people in heaven who remind Him of Jesus Christ.

Can you see why I say Jesus Christ is the centerpiece of God's program? Anything we say about prophecy in this book must be related to Christ to be properly focused.

JESUS CHRIST IS THE CAUSE OF PROPHECY

All of this raises a question: Why did God craft this plan, before there was ever a creation, to redeem a portion of humanity by His sovereign choice and present these people as a gift to His Son? A lot is mystery here, because we were not present when the Trinity held its eternal council. But at least part of the answer goes back to another event that took place before creation—the rebellion of the angel Lucifer in heaven and his judgment by God. The rebellion of this angelic being who became Satan led to God's gift of Christ to a redeemed humanity.

Part of my objective in setting the stage for our study of prophecy is to show you how Jesus Christ came to be the key and the focus of God's prophetic program. To see this, we must understand how the conflict between God and Satan developed and progressed.

So we need to review some central biblical teaching on God's war with Satan. This material is also important because Satan will appear again and again on the prophetic stage since the primary goal of his existence is to thwart the work of God and foil His plan for the consummation of this earth.

Lucifer's Exalted Status

Two major passages, Ezekiel 28 and Isaiah 14, introduce us to this angel called Lucifer who occupied a unique place in the heavenly realm. These chapters also describe his sin that led to open rebellion against God. We'll begin with Ezekiel 28. Ezekiel 28:12 says of Lucifer, "You had the seal of perfection, full of wisdom and perfect in beauty." This being was created flawless by God.

Lucifer also hung out in a perfect place. "Eden, the garden of God" (v. 13) may refer to an original Eden in heaven of which the garden of Eden on earth was a copy. This angel was a perfect being in a perfect location.

Lucifer's position was exalted too. As the "anointed cherub who covers" (v. 14), placed there by God, Lucifer was the head angel. He was God's showroom piece, His chief of staff. He led all the myriads of angels in the worship and adoration of God. He was the greatest of all God's created beings.

Lucifer's Terrible Downfall

But Lucifer's great beauty and exalted status were his downfall. They led him into pride. "Your heart was lifted up because of your beauty; you corrupted your wisdom by reason of your splendor" (Ezek. 28:17). In other words, Lucifer forgot he was created, not the Creator.

He began to think he had made himself powerful. He thought he had anointed himself as cherub. Lucifer forgot he was a creature totally dependent upon God for his glory, his beauty, his clout, his recognition, his awesomeness. And his heart was lifted up with pride, the greatest sin of all.

There is no sin worse than pride because all other sins come from it. Lucifer looked in the mirror and said, "Look how beautiful and how powerful I am. I don't need God. I can pull this thing off myself."

Lucifer's arrogance reminds me of the army officer who had just been promoted to general way before the creation of cellphones. He had gotten a new office, and was feeling very important. So when someone opened his office door to tell him a soldier was outside waiting to see him, the general decided to strut his stuff.

The general told the soldier to wait at the door as he picked up the telephone and said loudly, "Yes, Mr. President. I understand, Mr. President. I'll take care of it right away, Mr. President. You can count on me, Mr. President."

Then the general hung up the phone and asked the soldier what he wanted. "Well, sir, I'm here to hook up the telephone."

The Reasons for Lucifer's Fall

This was Lucifer when he became filled with pride. The point at which he became Satan is detailed further in Isaiah 14, where this exalted being made five "I will" pronouncements in rebellion against God. We'll review them briefly as we set the backdrop for the central place Christ holds in prophecy. Verse 12 describes Satan's fall and judgment, and then in verses 13–14 we find the reasons for his fall.

His first rebellious statement was "I will ascend to heaven." Satan wanted to take God's *position*. He was determined to occupy the very throne of God, to sit where God sits. Satan wanted it to be *his* heaven.

Second, he declared, "I will raise my throne above the stars of God." ("Stars" here are angels.) He also wanted to usurp God's *pre-eminence*. Satan said, "I'm tired of relaying God's commands to the other angels and making sure His orders are carried out. I want to be the one giving the orders. I want the other angels obeying me."

Satan's third statement was "I will sit on the mount of assembly." He wanted to share God's *power*. The word *mount* in the Bible is used of kingdoms. Satan wanted to sit at the center of God's kingdom rule. He didn't want to execute the plan; he wanted to make the plan.

A fourth desire of Satan's was "I will ascend above the heights of the clouds." Clouds in the Bible refer to God's glory, so Satan wanted to rob God of His *praise*. This angelic being wanted the glory and the worship that ascended to God to flow his way.

This proud boast reminds us of Jesus' temptation, when Satan showed Him all the world's kingdoms and then said, "All these things I will give You, if You fall down and worship me" (Matt. 4:8–9).

Fifth and finally, in Isaiah 14:14, Satan boasted, "I will make myself like the Most High." This is sort of a summary statement. Satan wanted to share God's *prerogatives*, the privileges and qualities God enjoys as the Sovereign of the universe. In particular, Satan desperately wanted to be independent of God. Satan saw that God was the only person in heaven who did not have to answer to *anybody*— and he wanted that same kind of total independence.

Yet Satan didn't get what he hoped for. Instead, he was judged for his rebellion. He was expelled from heaven and consigned to eternal punishment (see Matt. 25:41), a sentence that will be carried out as the last stages of God's prophetic plan are unveiled.

The Connection to Prophecy

How does the rebellion of Satan tie together with Jesus' central place in prophecy? The Bible declares that Jesus was revealed to "destroy the works of the devil" (1 John 3:8). In reference to Satan's judgment, Jesus said, "I was watching Satan fall from heaven like lightning" (Luke 10:18).

A trial was held in heaven in which Satan and his demons were found guilty of cosmic treason, rebellion against God. Jesus was saying, "I was at the trial when Satan was judged." Jesus saw Satan booted out of heaven "like lightning." The trial didn't last long, and the sentence was carried out in a hurry.

When he was convicted, the devil also got a name change. He who was Lucifer, "shining one," became Satan, the "adversary." Whenever God changes someone's name in the Bible, it's to reflect that person's character. *Satan* was the right name for God's adversary.

When Satan was kicked out of heaven, he took up temporary residence on the earth. His presence is evident from the fact that the earth was "formless and void, and darkness was over the surface of the deep" (Gen. 1:2). The earth became a garbage dump, because wherever Satan lives, he produces garbage.

God allowed Satan to inhabit the earth instead of just throwing him immediately into hell because the Trinity got together and made a decision. We don't know if this meeting was held before or after Satan actually rebelled, because as we said in the previous chapter, time distinctions are meaningless to God. Past, present, and future are the same to Him.

The important thing is that the Godhead decided to use Satan for a very crucial purpose. God the Father said to Jesus Christ, "My Son, Satan's rebellion and judgment present an opportunity to accomplish two very important purposes.

"To show You how much I love You, I am going to create mankind, a race of beings inferior to Satan and the angels. Satan will mess with these beings and try to get them to follow him. I will redeem from this race a body of humanity I am going to give You as My love gift to You. And I am going to redeem these people right out of the hand of Satan.

"This redemption will bring Me eternal glory. It will prove that I can take mankind, the lesser creature, and do more with lesser beings who obey Me than I can do with angels who rebel against Me. My second purpose is to demonstrate to the angels and all of creation what happens when anyone rebels against Me. I am going to allow Satan to continue his operations on earth, and yet in the end I will utterly defeat him and his associates and gain the final victory for all eternity." God's prophetic program is His response to Satan's rebellion.

What happens when the smoke of the final battle clears, when every prophetic event in the Bible has been fulfilled and time is no more? Jesus Christ has His redeemed throng rejoicing with Him forever in heaven, and Satan is totally defeated and thrown into the lake of fire.

Giving It All Back to God

Let me show you one more thing before we move on. Paul wrote of the final resurrection, "Then comes the end, when [Jesus] hands over the kingdom to the God and Father, when He has abolished all rule and all authority and power. . . . When all things are subjected to Him, then the Son Himself also will be subjected to the One who subjected all things to Him, so that God may be all in all" (1 Cor. 15:24, 28).

Guess what God is going to do? When His program for this earth is finished, when the goal of defeating Satan and redeeming a special people for His Son has been achieved, when Christ has ruled in His millennial kingdom, then the Son is going to say, "Father, You have loved Me so much to give Me this. Now let Me show My love to You by giving it all back to You."

When it's all over and eternity is ushered in, God will be all in all. There is such an equality of love and equality of essence between the Father and the Son that they will share equally in the fruit of the prophetic plan that was conceived before the world began.

JESUS CHRIST IS THE CONTENT OF PROPHECY

There is no question that Jesus is the centerpiece of prophecy. And He is the cause of prophecy in the sense that the purpose of God's plan was to present a gift of redeemed humanity to His Son.

Jesus is also the content, the subject, of prophecy. There's no guess-work about this either, because we have Jesus' word on it. He said so Himself to two of His discouraged disciples on the road to a little village called Emmaus.

Missing the Message

You probably know this story well. It's a familiar account in Luke, occurring at evening of the most important day in history, the day of Christ's resurrection. The two disciples were returning home discouraged because they didn't believe the reports that Jesus had risen. Jesus joined them on the road, although they didn't recognize Him.

When Jesus asked the two what they were discussing, they explained that it concerned "Jesus the Nazarene, who was a prophet mighty in deed and word in the sight of God and all the people" (Luke 24:19). They went on to explain that they had hoped this Jesus would be Israel's Messiah. But since He had been crucified, and since it was now the third day since His death, they figured they had been wrong, and they were heading home.

This is amazing unbelief on the part of these two disciples, considering they also told Jesus all about the women's reports of the empty tomb and how other disciples had checked it out (vv. 22–24). They apparently did not believe the reports.

Jesus in the Old Testament

No wonder Jesus said to them, "O foolish men and slow of heart to believe in all that the prophets have spoken! Was it not necessary for the Christ to suffer these things and to enter into His glory?" (Luke 24:25–26).

And then, "Beginning with Moses and with all the prophets, He explained to them the things concerning Himself in all the Scriptures" (v. 27). This is a very important verse, because it's here that Jesus demonstrated to these two men how He was the subject of all the prophetic Scripture.

"Moses and the prophets" was another term for the Old Testament. Moses takes us all the way back to the beginning and the first five books of the Bible. Jesus was saying that Moses talked about Him, the writers in the poetic books talked about Him, and the prophets talked about Him.

But Jesus wasn't born until after all the Old Testament writers were long gone from the scene. So what does that make their writings about His coming? Prophecy. Jesus showed these men that the Old Testament was all about Him.

All the sacrifices offered in the Old Testament were made in anticipation of the coming Lamb of God. The Levitical priesthood was all about the High Priest who was to come. The Old Testament prophets came to foreshadow the Prophet who would come someday (see Deut. 18:15). The kings of Israel pointed forward to the coming King of kings.

I'm sure Jesus also took them to Psalm 22 and the prophecy of His crucifixion, and mentioned Psalm 16, which prophesies His resurrection. He probably pointed them to Isaiah 9:6, the prophecy of the Child who would be born. The entire Old Testament is about Christ.

Fellowship with Christ

If you don't see Christ, you become spiritually blind, like these disciples were that night on the Emmaus road. And when you become spiritually blind, circumstances rule your emotions. That was their problem. They were depressed because they thought their Messiah was gone, yet He was walking with them.

So Jesus gave these two an unforgettable Bible study as they walked along. Notice Luke 24:28–29: "They approached the village where they were going, and He acted as though He were going farther. But they urged Him, saying, 'Stay with us.'"

Why did Jesus act as if He was going to keep going when they arrived at Emmaus? Why did He give the two disciples an opening to invite Him to stay with them? I think Jesus was testing them to see what they were going to do with what they had heard. He had just taught them everything the Old Testament had to say about Himself. Would they invite Him in?

Jesus Christ is doing the same with us today. If I am not going to do anything with Jesus, He will skip my house and come to your house. That's why some believers are further ahead than other believers in their Christian lives. Some people come to church and hear the truth, but then they allow Jesus just to keep on walking right by them. In fact, when they get into their cars after church and head home, Jesus is heading in the other direction because there is no invitation for Him to fellowship with them.

Remember, God doesn't want you to learn prophecy so you can know facts and argue the points. He wants you to learn prophecy so He can fellowship with you around the truth of His Word, so you can be intimate with Him as you look forward to all that will unfold in the days to come. The content, the point, of prophecy is Jesus Christ.

Jesus accepted the offer from the disciples and sat down with them. As soon as He had broken bread, they recognized Him, and He disappeared from their sight (Luke 24:30–31). "They said to one another, 'Were not our hearts burning within us while He was speaking to us on the road, while He was explaining the Scriptures to us?'" (v. 32).

Don't miss the sequence of events here. Even though Jesus had taught them a wonderful "series" on prophecy, they didn't get the message until they sought fellowship with the Teacher. If you miss Jesus, you have missed everything.

JESUS CHRIST IS THE CULMINATION OF PROPHECY

As we consider our fourth and final point, I want to turn to Ephesians 1, where we read, "[God] made known to us the mystery of His will . . . with a view to an administration suitable to the fulness of the times, that is, the summing up of all things in Christ, things in the heavens and things on the earth" (vv. 9–10).

Clearly, the culmination of God's program is found in the person and work of Jesus Christ. We saw that God's plan started with Christ in the councils of eternity, and it is going to end with Christ. Every knee is going to bow at the name of Jesus (see Phil. 2:10).

The Climax of God's Program

The book of Revelation, which describes the culmination of God's prophetic program, opens with this declaration: "The Revelation of Jesus Christ" (Rev. 1:1). This book, with all that it has to say about the future, is fundamentally about Him.

Then Christ made this statement: "I am the Alpha and the Omega . . . who is and who was and who is to come" (v. 8). Alpha and omega are the first and last letters of the Greek alphabet, so Jesus was saying He is the whole show. All things climax, or culminate, in Him.

Therefore, we can say that prophecy is about the exaltation, glorification, and adoration of Jesus Christ. God has placed all of history in the lap of Jesus Christ. And that's why to miss the Son is to miss the point of everything, including life itself.

The Subject of Our Praise

If all of history culminates in Jesus Christ, that means you and I had better be directing all our praise to Him. Later in the Revelation, John said:

I looked, and behold, a great multitude which no one could count, from every nation and all tribes and peoples and tongues, standing before the throne and before the Lamb, clothed in white robes, and palm branches were in their hands; and they cry out with a loud voice, saying,

"Salvation to our God who sits on the throne, and to the Lamb." And all the angels were standing around the throne and around the elders and the four living creatures; and they fell on their faces before the throne and worshiped God. (Rev. 7:9–11)

This is quite a picture of praise. Redeemed people from every corner of the earth, the myriads of angels, and the special beings in heaven whose job is to praise God were all gathered before God the Father and Jesus the Lamb, pouring forth their praise and adoration.

What is the culmination of prophecy going to be like? The council meeting of the Godhead that began before history is going to end with God the Father saying to Jesus, "Son, I love You. You are the apple of My eye. To let You know how much I love You, I have created for You a redeemed humanity. And so that You will never forget how much I love You, these redeemed people are going to sing Your praises for eternity."

God has created millions, and perhaps billions, of creatures who will sing praises to the Son. We who know Christ as our Savior will have the privilege of being in this eternal choir. If we are going to be singing the praises of Jesus Christ in heaven for all eternity, doesn't it make sense that we should be getting our voices in practice down here? He is the culmination, the capstone, of God's program—and the object of His Father's attention and love.

So as we look at the details of prophecy, it's okay to get excited about them as you see the things predicted in the Old Testament coming true in the New Testament, and as you see the wonderful future God has prepared for His own.

But in your excitement, and in your study, don't miss Jesus. Because to miss Jesus is to miss the real excitement. Jesus Christ is the key to prophecy.

3

PROPHECY AND HUMAN HISTORY

Most people are familiar enough with the Shakespearean play *Romeo and Juliet* to know that it is a love story about two teenagers that ends in tragedy. But you can only fully appreciate the tragedy behind *Romeo and Juliet* if you understand the backdrop against which their love occurred. This is a story of the conflict between the Montagues and the Capulets, two families locked in a bitter feud.

The problem was that Romeo was a Montague, and Juliet was a Capulet, so their love was doomed from the beginning. Their families would never grant them permission to marry, so the tragic tale unfolded against the larger backdrop of family warfare that eventually helped to decide the fate of the main characters in the story.

What's true of *Romeo and Juliet* is also true of human history. To understand where the human race has been, where we are today, and where we are going, we must see human history against the backdrop of the angelic conflict we examined in the previous chapter.

As we saw in that overview, Satan rebelled against God, was judged for his pride, and was expelled from heaven. But instead of carrying out Satan's eternal punishment immediately, God banished the devil and his rebellious angelic followers to the lower portion of His creation, planet earth and the atmospheric heavens surrounding the earth. God also decided in the counsel of the Trinity to use the rebellion of Satan for a greater purpose, the demonstration of His glory for all the angelic world and all of creation to see.

God determined to save lost people so that He could present a redeemed race to His Son as a love gift. The redemption of mankind was the greatest manifestation of God's glory, so these purposes are closely intertwined. But the greater, overarching purpose is the glory of God.

The way God chose to manifest His glory was by creating human beings, creatures inferior to Satan and the angels. Then God decided to create a brief space between eternity past and eternity future called time, or history, and place mankind and Satan in this interlude.

The unfolding of human history, then, is the outworking of God's plan to demonstrate His glory and defeat Satan forever using lesser creatures, human beings, who would serve and obey Him. We're going to see how biblical prophecy ties into this, because the Bible's earliest prophecy occurs in connection with the dawn of human history.

THE CREATION OF MAN

David addressed the reason for our creation in Psalm 8. After asking the question, "What is man that You take thought of him?" (v. 4), David answered in these classic verses:

> Yet You have made him a little lower than God ["the angels" KJV],
> And You crown him with glory and majesty!
> You make him to rule over the works of Your hands;
> You have put all things under his feet. (vv. 5–6)

Our Position in Creation

I believe David was talking about our position in relation to the angels, not to God, despite the New American Standard reading here. Although we are "a little lower" than the angels in their intrinsic being as eternal creatures, we were created to rule over all creation— including angels—on God's behalf.

The writer of Hebrews confirmed this view when he quoted Psalm 8 and said mankind was created "a little while lower than the angels" (Heb. 2:7). Then he added, "For in subjecting all things to him, He [God] left nothing that is not subject to him" (v. 8).

Why was mankind created inferior to the angels? So God could get greater glory in our redemption—because when the lesser defeats the greater, then He gets all the praise.

In fact, this has been God's way of operating throughout history. God sent a David to kill a Goliath. Tiny Israel routed larger and more powerful enemies. Paul told the Corinthians, "Consider your calling, brethren, that there were not many wise according to the flesh, not many mighty, not many noble; but God has chosen the foolish things of the world to shame the wise" (1 Cor. 1:26–27).

That's why the lower you go, the more God can use you. But the higher you get, the more He has to humble you. The Bible says, "Humble yourselves under the mighty hand of God, that He may exalt you at the proper time" (1 Peter 5:6).

The Act of Creation

We'll spend the rest of this chapter in the opening chapters of Genesis, looking briefly at the creation account as the beginning of human history and the setting for the beginning of the cosmic conflict between God and Satan. Man's creation was first recorded in Genesis 1:26. "Then God said, 'Let Us make man in Our image, according to Our likeness.'" Verse 27 then describes the fulfillment of God's intention. "God created man in His own image, in the image of God He created him; male and female He created them."

The fact that we are created in God's image and likeness is very important. Since it cannot refer to our physical makeup, it means we are created with the attributes of intellect, emotion, and volition or will, just as God has these attributes. We bear the image or stamp of God in our souls and spirits.

We are also like God in our ability to produce new life. The first thing God said to His new creatures was, "Be fruitful and multiply" (Gen. 1:28). Adam and Eve were also told to "subdue" and "rule over" the earth (v. 28). That is, they were to rule as God's representatives on the earth, which was Satan's domain. Here we can see God's purpose of bringing glory to Himself by demonstrating what He can do with the lesser creation, man.

A Reminder of Creation

God placed one tree in the middle of the garden of Eden and commanded Adam and Eve concerning it, "From the tree of the knowledge of good and evil you will not eat, for in the day that you eat from it you will surely die" (Gen. 2:17).

Why did God do that? Because the tree in the middle of the garden was there to remind Adam and Eve of their creatureliness. It was a reminder that they were the created ones, not the Creator. It served notice that some things were off-limits; there were some things they couldn't do, some prerogatives they didn't have.

The Tree of the Knowledge of Good and Evil was a daily reminder that it was God who set the rules in the garden. The prohibition on eating from it was a statement that God never wants knowledge to be investigated independently of Him—which is exactly what we have today in the heresy of humanism.

Another tree in Eden was called the Tree of Life. Adam and Eve were free to eat from it. These two trees were probably right next to each other, presenting mankind with a clear choice. Would it be obedience, or rebellion and disobedience like Satan?

THE COLLAPSE OF MAN

In Genesis 3, human history took a terrible plunge downward, appropriately called the fall. This pivotal chapter is actually the beginning of prophecy, because from the moment Adam and Eve rebelled and sinned against God, the divine plan has been focused on the battle between God and Satan and God's ultimate triumph.

The drama began with the arrival of another character on the scene. "Now the serpent was more crafty than any beast of the field which the LORD God had made" (v. 1).

This was Satan's first recorded appearance on earth after being expelled from heaven. He was going to work through a snake to tempt Eve and find out whether she would obey God or rebel and follow him. He was going to smooth talk her into sin.

Focusing on the Prohibition

Satan's approach was to focus on the one prohibition God had made in the midst of all the abundance of Eden. God had commanded Adam not to eat from the Tree of the Knowledge of Good and Evil, under penalty of death (Gen. 2:17). So the serpent asked Eve, "Indeed, has God said, 'You shall not eat from any tree of the garden'?" (3:1).

Satan knew what God had said to Adam and Eve about the trees in the garden. The devil brought up that conversation because he knew he had to get God's command out of Eve's mind if he was going to seduce her.

Satan cannot defeat the Word of God. But he can manipulate us so that we begin to doubt or disregard the Word, and when that happens, he can defeat us. You don't have to deny the Word to get in trouble. All you have to do is ignore it. Thus, Satan was going to start messing with Eve's mind.

In answer to the serpent's question, Eve said, "From the fruit of the trees of the garden we may eat; but from the fruit of the tree which is in the middle of the garden, God has said, 'You shall not eat from it or touch it, or you will die'" (Gen. 3:2–3).

We have two problems here already. First, Eve should have been emphasizing to the serpent the hundreds of trees they *were* free to eat from. She mentioned that fact, but her focus wasn't on God's goodness because as soon as the serpent pointed to the one forbidden tree, she got hung up on it.

Someone has said that even God's negative commands imply a positive side. His "thou shalt nots" mean there are a lot of other things we can do. Don't let Satan trick you into thinking *I can't do that* and get you upset over the one thing you can't do so you don't enjoy the five hundred things you can do.

A second problem here is that Eve didn't quote God's command correctly. She left out a crucial word God said, added another idea He didn't say, and weakened the consequences of His command.

God had said to Adam, "From any tree of the garden you may eat *freely*" (Gen. 2:16, italics added). The point is that God didn't just provide for Adam; He provided *abundantly*. This was God's grace, at no cost to Adam. Eve missed that, and Satan got her to thinking what a miserly God she had because He was holding out on her.

Eve also added to God's prohibition. She told the serpent God commanded her not even to *touch* the forbidden tree. But God didn't say that. So again, she was making God look narrow and restrictive and harsh and legalistic.

Eve also failed to mention the absolute certainty of the penalty for disobeying God. She said, "You will die." But God had said, "You will *surely* die" (v. 17, italics added).

Denying God's Word

These little subtleties crept into Eve's conversation with the devil and God's Word was weakened. Satan jumped on the opportunity and came out with a flat denial of that Word. "The serpent said to the woman, 'You surely will not die! For God knows that in the day you eat from it your eyes will be opened, and you will be like God, knowing good and evil'" (Gen. 3:4–5).

Now Satan's attack went frontal. He was telling Eve she was not obligated to do what God said because God had an ulterior motive. Not only did Satan call God a liar, but he accused God of holding out on Adam and Eve.

Satan was saying to Eve, "Let me tell you something about God. He doesn't want anyone else trying to be like Him. He knows that if you eat of this tree you will be like Him, and He's so jealous and so stingy with His deity that He won't share it with anyone else."

Well, Satan was right on that one. God will not share His deity or His glory with anyone. But Satan lied about the consequences of disobeying God. Death, not deity, awaited Adam and Eve if they disobeyed.

A Deceptive Offer

Now Satan made Eve an enticing offer. Since God was holding out on her and Adam, Satan implied, and since they couldn't really enjoy life to its fullest under God's restriction, Satan offered to help Eve get all she deserved. He made the forbidden tree look all the more appealing. "When the woman saw that the tree was good for food, and that it was a delight to the eyes, and that the tree was desirable to make one wise, she took from its fruit and ate; and she gave also to her husband with her, and he ate" (Gen. 3:6).

The problem was that Eve allowed her emotions to overrule God's revelation. She looked at the tree and got all tingly. It looked good, and the idea of being like God sounded good, so she rebelled against God. Eve substituted personal desire for objective truth, and she paid the price. And Adam followed right along with her.

Remember, we're setting the scene for the first and most basic statement of biblical prophecy. Once Adam and Eve fell, the stage was set for the contest between God and Satan that would last throughout human history and take Jesus to the cross.

THE CONFLICT OVER MAN

The fall of Adam and Eve brings us to the verse we've been referring to, what I'm calling the conflict over mankind and his eternal destiny.

In the process of judging the serpent, God said, "I will put enmity between you and the woman, and between your seed and her seed; he shall bruise you on the head, and you shall bruise him on the heel" (Gen. 3:15).

This is the Bible's first prophecy, and it contains the basic outcome of God's prophetic drama. Satan's seed, those opposed to God, would deliver a crippling blow to Christ, the seed of a woman named Mary, on the cross (the bruise on the heel).

However, Christ would ultimately deliver a *fatal* blow to Satan (the bruise on the head). Part of this blow came when Jesus Christ rose from the dead, redeeming mankind and guaranteeing Satan's eternal judgment. God used this prophecy to explain the conflict that was about to unfold in human history and that is still in progress today. This important verse is prophetic because God was talking about the Seed, or offspring, who had not yet come.

So this was all future. In fact, part of it is still future today because Satan has not yet been finally and fully destroyed. Let's notice some important things about Genesis 3:15.

God's "I Will" Statement

The first thing I want you to notice is God's declaration, "I will . . ." Does that sound familiar? It should. We've seen that Lucifer made this same statement five times in Isaiah 14 as he declared his rebellion against God. But the moment the devil exercised his independent, rebellious will, he lost and got booted out of heaven. But when God says, "I will," nothing can stop Him. The triumph of His will is being worked out in history, and we can watch it unfold through prophecy.

Satan could say what he would do, but he couldn't guarantee it. That's the problem with following Satan. He can talk a better game than he can deliver. But God makes it very clear in this declaration that He is the One setting the conditions of the conflict that commenced in Eden and is being carried on in history.

God gave Satan an edge, as it were, by saying, "I am going to judge you, Satan, but not directly. I am going to do it through the seed of the woman, a person who will deliver you a fatal blow."

Notice that God said this coming Man would be the seed of a woman. In normal human conception, it is a man's seed that produces a baby as it fertilizes the woman's egg. But not so in this case. No human father was involved, because God was speaking prophetically of His Son, Jesus Christ, who was born of a virgin.

The War in History

So the battle was on, and all of history is now the outworking of this struggle. What we will see from this point on is the unfolding of prophecy as it relates to the fulfillment of the Bible's first great prophecy—the earthly life, death, and triumphant return of Jesus Christ.

The human race was at the center of this cosmic conflict because the heart of the battle is the question of who will win mankind's allegiance.

Satan had encroached upon the territory of God's glory and wanted to claim it for himself. And Satan was trying to bring with him a host of beings, both angelic and human, to lay claim to territory that belongs to God alone.

But God said, "I will have My seed who will respond to the rebellion of Satan." We are part of that seed as the children of God who have sworn allegiance to Him. But as we said, the ultimate seed is Jesus Himself.

A Gracious Guard

After God had expelled a sinful Adam and Eve from the garden, "He stationed the cherubim and the flaming sword which turned every direction to guard the way to the tree of life" (Gen. 3:24). This was a very gracious thing God did, because if Adam and Eve had eaten from the Tree of Life in their sinful condition, they would have lived forever in their sin and under God's judgment. So God had to keep mankind away from the tree until He could provide the way of salvation.

The Next Generation

It didn't take long to see this conflict between God and Satan really break out. Adam and Eve had their first two children, Cain and Abel (Gen. 4:1–2). And "in the course of time," as Cain's offering was rejected by God while Abel's was accepted, that evil Cain killed righteous Abel (vv. 3–8).

So here was Cain operating under Satan's influence, attempting to wipe out God's righteous seed before it even had a chance to become established. As we will see, attempting to destroy God's seed has been the focus of Satan's program throughout history.

Even though Cain fell under Satan's influence, Cain used religion to try and make himself acceptable to God. Religion is trying to please God on your terms. Cain brought an offering to God, but it wasn't the offering God required. Religion is man's attempt to make his own way to God, as opposed to salvation, which is coming to God on His terms, in His way based on His Word.

THE CONQUEST BY A MAN

The human race may have collapsed into sin and been conquered by Satan, but there's one Man whom Satan could not defeat.

Before we move on, I want you to see the moment of conquest when the seed of the woman, Jesus Christ, delivered the crushing, fatal blow to Satan. Once that death blow was delivered, the rest of the conflict is just a mopping up operation.

The Right Man at the Right Time

Galatians 4:4 is a great summary of what happened in history when God's program of crushing Satan was fulfilled. "When the fulness of the time came, God sent forth His Son, born of a woman, born under the Law."

Jesus came at just the right time in history. You have probably heard it said this way: He may not come when you want Him to come, but He is always on time. When all the factors of history had come together to make it the right time, God sent Jesus Christ to be born of a virgin. Jesus came under the Law, the Old Testament system of sacrifices God put in place temporarily after the fall of man, because Jesus was the fulfillment of that Old Testament system. He was the final sacrifice toward which all the Old Testament sacrifices pointed.

Jesus Christ came for this express purpose: "To destroy the works of the devil" (1 John 3:8). He accomplished that purpose on the cross. Because of His conquest, when we put our faith in Him we regain our original created purpose, which, as we learned in Psalm 8, is to rule over God's creation.

Satan's Defeat at the Cross

Satan knew he had to get rid of Christ. He tried to kill Him as a baby when Herod had the baby boys of Bethlehem put to death. Then Satan tried to get Jesus to fall in the wilderness temptation.

Neither of those worked, but Satan must have thought he had reached his goal when he inspired wicked people to crucify Jesus on the cross. Satan did not know that the cross was going to be the instrument of Jesus' triumph over him. Paul wrote in Colossians 2:13–14 that Jesus canceled our sin debt at the cross by shedding His blood to pay for sin. Then he continued, "When [God] had disarmed the rulers and authorities, He made a public display of them, having triumphed over them through [Christ]" (v. 15).

That's the critical verse. Satan was disarmed at the cross; his weapons were rendered useless at Calvary. The cross was the defining moment in history, when Christ defeated Satan.

Satan defeated Adam and Eve because they sinned. And Satan can defeat you and me because we are sinful too. Satan thought he had control of the human race because all have sinned. But Satan didn't bank on the fact that God would deal with sin through the cross. All of our sins were laid to the account of Jesus Christ, and Jesus paid it all.

Not only that, but God laid to our account the righteousness of Christ. This is because Jesus not only died on the cross, but He also lived a perfect life. God credited Jesus' righteousness to our account, so that we have not only the removal of sin, but we have Christ's righteousness put in its place on our account ledger.

Our Conquest in Christ

The writer to the Hebrews said this of Jesus Christ: "We do see Him who was made for a little while lower than the angels, namely, Jesus, because of the suffering of death crowned with glory and honor, so that by the grace of God He might taste death for everyone" (Heb. 2:9).

In other words, because you and I are human, God had to become a human to save us. Christ had to die for our sin because God's righteousness demanded payment for sin. But in His death Jesus was able to "render powerless him who had the power of death, that is, the devil, and might free those who through fear of death were subject to slavery all their lives" (Heb. 2:14–15).

Follow the reasoning here. Since Satan was rendered powerless at the cross, the only power he has in the lives of Christians is the power we let him have. Sometimes we say, "I wish Satan would get off my back." But Dr. Martin Luther King Jr. reminded us that a person can only ride your back if your back is bent. Satan only has the control over you that you surrender to him. But he cannot handle the cross of Christ. That's why we need to see Jesus.

We are the victors over Satan in Christ, but activating our victory requires something of us. In Revelation 12:11 we are given a three-fold means for conquering Satan. Looking ahead into the future, this verse says, "They overcame him [the devil] because of the blood of the Lamb and because of the word of their testimony, and they did not love their life even when faced with death." This verse simply means that these believers lived their lives based upon the accomplishment of Christ. They had the cross, which gave them the power to make their confession and hold to their commitment.

That's what we need today to defeat Satan. Even though we may not face their test of martyrdom, when you hold up the cross in the devil's face, he can't overcome that. He has to flee. The blood of the Lamb has conquered Satan.

Part of holding up the cross is our public confession and testimony of Christ. And when that confession comes together with a commitment to Christ that is greater than our desire even to live, we have some powerful weapons to use on the devil (Zech. 3:1–10). When you confess Christ and His cross, you will beat Satan every time. He will have no more authority in your life. So while we are waiting for the future realization of Christ's full and final conquest of Satan, we can experience that victory now because of the cross.

I like what Paul told the Romans: "The God of peace will soon crush Satan under your feet" (Rom. 16:20). Though this hasn't happened yet, you're still dealing with a defeated enemy. Christ is already victor over Satan because of the cross. If you are a child of God, Satan should not be stepping on you anymore. He should be dust under your feet.

How could that be possible? Because "God has chosen the weak things of the world to shame the things which are strong" (1 Cor. 1:27). He has chosen to take weak bundles of human flesh like us and put us up against the mightiest of the angels, Satan, to demonstrate what He can do with a lesser creature who will obey Him.

God has chosen to do things this way because He gets the greater glory when we conquer sin and Satan in His power. And we give God all the glory because we know it was "'not by might nor by power, but by My Spirit,' says the LORD of hosts" (Zech. 4:6).

4

PROPHECY AND THE COVENANTS

If you have ever signed a contract to buy a house or a car, or if you have said "I do" with the confirmation of a minister, then you have the basic biblical concept of a *covenant*. The history of the Bible is linked together by covenants, as we will see in this chapter. In fact, one of the key ways to identify the unfolding of Bible prophecy is through the covenants God makes with people.

A covenant is a relationship or agreement between God and His people in terms of the plan of action God is going to follow to carry out His program. In short, I define a covenant as a *spiritually binding relationship between God and you inclusive of certain agreements, conditions, benefits, responsibilities, and effects.*

All of the biblical covenants that are important for prophecy were initiated by God, and in the sense that they are God's statements of what He is going to do, they were prophetic or predictive at the time they were made.

It's also important to mention up front that whenever God makes a covenant, we can rest assured that He will fulfill His word. A

51

covenant is only as good as the people making it. When God enters into a covenant, He brings to it His perfect character. In fact, the Bible often refers to God as a God who keeps His promises or His covenants (Deut. 7:9; Heb. 10:23).

Before we get into the major covenants and their relationship to the unfolding of prophecy, let me briefly point out several examples of biblical covenants. The Mosaic Law referred to a "covenant of salt" (Num. 18:19; see Lev. 2:13) in relation to Israel's grain offerings.

There is no indication of any formal agreement process in this covenant. The sprinkling of salt on the sacrifices suggested permanence and preservation, the qualities of salt. The grain thus salted was also preserved for the Levites as their part of the offerings.

An example of a covenant between two people is found in Ruth 4:7–9, where Boaz accepted the sandal of his relative as a sign that this man was handing over to Boaz the right to redeem the inheritance of Elimelech, who had died, and the right to marry Ruth. The sandal was the equivalent of a signed contract.

The most serious covenant of all is the covenant ratified by blood, of which there are several examples in Scripture. The earliest of these covenants is the Adamic covenant, in which God killed animals in order to cover Adam and Eve and then promised that a future Redeemer would come to crush Satan (Gen. 3:15).

THE COVENANT WITH NOAH

In the previous chapter, we looked at the murder of Abel by his brother Cain, the next step in the battle between the seed of God and the seed of Satan (Gen. 4:1–8).

This act of violence set a tone of evil that escalated the battle until wickedness dominated the earth. God moved decisively to deal with this intolerable situation, and in the process of bringing worldwide judgment He also established a covenant with Noah that is still in effect.

The Domination of Evil

The "sons of God," a group of the fallen angels who followed Satan in his rebellion, infiltrated the human race by using unrighteous men to have illicit sexual relationships with women and producing a demonic seed (Gen. 6:1–4). This pollution of the race was enough to bring God's judgment, so we read this declaration:

> The LORD saw that the wickedness of man was great on the earth, and that every intent of the thoughts of his heart was only evil continually. The LORD was sorry that He had made man on the earth, and He was grieved in His heart. The LORD said, "I will blot out man whom I have created . . . for I am sorry that I have made them." (vv. 5–7)

God determined to judge mankind with the flood because the human race was contaminated by this demonic seed produced through the unrighteous. However, "Noah found favor in the eyes of the LORD" (v. 8). Noah was a righteous man, and he became the one through whom God would continue the human race and preserve the righteous seed.

So God sent the flood to cover the earth, with only Noah and his family being saved. For our purposes here, we need to look at what happened after the flood when Noah left the ark. The first thing he did was build an altar to worship the Lord (Gen. 8:20).

The Promise of the Covenant

God smelled the "soothing aroma" of Noah's sacrifice and made an unconditional, unilateral promise—or covenant—never to destroy the entire earth by water again (Gen. 8:21–22). God also made some other promises and stipulations in this covenant He was making with Noah. Specifically, God promised ample provisions for Noah. And

He established the principle of the sacredness of human life by requiring the death penalty for anyone who committed murder.

Then God ratified the covenant by saying, "Now behold, I Myself do establish My covenant with you, and with your descendants after you" (Gen. 9:9). Again, God said, "I establish My covenant with you; and all flesh shall never again be cut off by the water of the flood, neither shall there again be a flood to destroy the earth" (v. 11).

Then God gave Noah a sign of the covenant, which was the rainbow that we can still see today. Every time you see a rainbow, it is a reminder of God's promise that there will never again be a worldwide flood to destroy the earth. The Noahic covenant is an "everlasting covenant," by the way (v. 16). It is still in effect, and will be as long as the earth remains.

In His covenant with Noah, God instituted human government for the first time. That's implied in the commandment to carry out capital punishment for murder. Noah and his descendants were charged with establishing righteousness in civilization through government, which was a new thing on the earth.

God also commanded Noah, "Be fruitful and multiply, and fill the earth" (Gen. 9:1), which is the same command He gave to Adam. God decided to start over with Noah, with the difference that instead of administering justice directly from above, God would deliver justice to the human race through the institution we call government. From then on, people would be responsible for the execution of God's righteousness on earth. This is why Paul called duly constituted government "a minister of God to you for good" (Rom. 13:4).

But mankind soon corrupted God's program as Nimrod led the world in rebellion against God at Babel (Gen. 10:8–10; 11:1–9), with the result that God judged the people and scattered them over the face of the earth.

Instead of sending another flood, which He had promised not to do, God confused people's language and set the stage for the introduction of what we know as "nationalism." That is, God set boundaries around the nations so they could no longer come together and seek unity independently of Him (Acts 17:26–27).

THE COVENANT WITH ABRAHAM

The rebellion of the nations at Babel produced a major shift in God's program. Whereas God had been dealing with mankind in general, beginning in the last portion of Genesis 11, He turned His attention to one man. And whereas God had been dealing with all the nations, He would now turn His attention to one special nation that would come from the seed of this one man, Abraham.

Through Abraham, God would raise up a special people, a unique nation He would call His own. And God began doing this when Abraham was a pagan man living in a pagan nation called "Ur of the Chaldeans" (Gen. 11:28). God called Abraham out of Ur and sent him to Canaan, where God would establish with him the foundational covenant in all the Bible.

God didn't ignore the other covenants, but the Abrahamic covenant became the central mechanism by which the rest of God's program would unfold and be measured.

The Covenant Promised

Genesis 11:31–32 records the beginning of Abraham's trek from Ur to Canaan. Evidently God had already called him to leave home and go to Canaan before we read about it in Genesis 12:1.

Abraham obeyed, but only partially, because the family settled in Haran. Abraham didn't receive the blessing or the covenant until he had fully obeyed and started out for Canaan. My point is that to enjoy the benefits of God's covenant, you can't stay in the old world, the old life.

God did not call Abraham to enter the promised land until his father, Terah, had died in Haran. God would not let Abraham take the old life into the new. It appears that Abraham clung to the old way of life while living in Haran as long as Terah was alive. He had to break with the old life in order to enter into the new life. We have to do the same today.

Once Terah had died, God called Abraham and gave him some incredible promises:

Now the LORD said to Abram,

"Go forth from your country,
And from your relatives
And from your father's house,
To the land which I will show you;
And I will make you a great nation,
And I will bless you,
And make your name great;
And so you shall be a blessing;
And I will bless those who bless you,
And the one who curses you I will curse.
And in you all the families of the earth will be blessed."
(Gen. 12:1–3)

God gave Abraham both personal and national promises that would later be ratified by God in a covenant ceremony. First of all, look at the personal promises. Abraham (still Abram at this time) would have a great name and great blessing from God. In fact, his new name (Gen. 17:5) was a witness to the blessings God had in store for him.

God also made the promise that Abraham would become the father of a great nation. This promise was restated at a later time, but here is the first prophecy of the birth of the nation of Israel, who would become God's chosen people.

This is important because the rest of human history, and prophetic history, would rotate around the axis of this nation that occupies a narrow strip of land in the Middle East. That's still happening today. History will find its culmination in the Middle East. If you want to know what God is doing from a prophetic standpoint, keep your eyes on Israel. Whenever disruptions occur in Israel, it draws the attention of the entire world, and for good reason.

Not too long ago, I was set to lead a tour of a thousand guests to visit Israel. We had tirelessly made plans over the course of the previous year and looked with great anticipation toward the trip. I had planned to preach at the various biblical sites, and I couldn't wait to fellowship with a thousand of our dear ministry friends traveling with us to Israel.

But war broke out only a few weeks before we were set to depart. As you might imagine, all eyes were on Israel. Country after country lit up their cities and state houses in blue and white to show solidarity. The news channels relayed the events in Israel almost nonstop. Even though Israel is a relatively small nation on the global scale, roughly the size of New Jersey, when war happens in Israel—it captures the attention of the world.

Sadly, yet understandably, we had to cancel our tour of the Holy Land as airlines began canceling their flights both into and out of the country. But our prayers remained fervent for those who were there and wanting to return to their home nations, as well as for those who lived there. Israel draws the hearts, minds, and thoughts of the world like no other nation has ever done before. Understanding prophecy helps explain why.

One reason is that Abraham's blessings go far beyond Abraham. His blessing even reaches international proportions, because God said that all the peoples of earth would be blessed through Abraham. You can see why the Abrahamic covenant is the foundational covenant of Scripture, and why so many people are interested in what happens in

Israel. This covenant's ultimate fulfillment is in Jesus Christ, which also makes it crucial.

At this point, Abraham probably didn't know what all of this meant or how all of it was going to be fulfilled. He was merely a converted pagan who had acted in faith and traveled to a barren, dusty land where he lived in tents.

This reminds us of the way God often works. He will not always tell you everything He's doing at the beginning of wherever He's taking you. He may give you a little bit now and a little bit later, and then a little more after that. That's why the Bible says, "We walk by faith, not by sight" (2 Cor. 5:7).

Abraham only received the promises after he stepped out in faith at God's command. He had to leave his home and his relatives. He could not simply sit in his home in Ur and say, "I trust You, Lord." He had to get up and leave.

So here we have this great man Abraham with these great promises. God repeated His covenant promises to Abraham time and again. One of these was in the very next chapter, Genesis 13. After Abraham had separated from his nephew Lot, allowing Lot to take the better-looking land, God said to Abraham:

> Now lift up your eyes and look from the place where you are, northward and southward and eastward and westward; for all the land which you see, I will give it to you and to your descendants forever. I will make your descendants as the dust of the earth, so that if anyone can number the dust of the earth, then your descendants can also be numbered. (Gen. 13:14–16)

Here was an important restatement of God's covenant promise at a critical point in Abraham's life, when it looked as if he had come out on the short end of the deal.

Another restatement of the promise comes in Genesis 17, which we'll mention here even though it takes us out of the biblical sequence. God said to Abraham:

> I will establish My covenant between Me and you, and I will multiply you exceedingly. . . . My covenant is with you, and you will be the father of a multitude of nations. . . . I will give to you and to your descendants after you, the land of your sojournings, all the land of Canaan, for an everlasting possession. (vv. 2, 4, 8)

The Covenant Ratified

Now we come to Genesis 15 and the actual ceremony by which God ratified His covenant with Abraham. Abraham had just defeated the federation of kings who had kidnapped Lot and his family. "After these things the word of the LORD came to Abram in a vision, saying, 'Do not fear, Abram, I am a shield to you; your reward shall be very great'" (v. 1).

In other words, "Keep trusting Me, Abraham." Don't just look for the signs or other things God gives; look for God. He is your reward, not anything else.

But Abraham saw a problem. "O Lord GOD, what will You give me, since I am childless?" (v. 2). That's a definite problem for a man who is supposed to have so many descendants they can't be counted.

Why would God promise to make a great nation out of an old man with a wife who couldn't have children (see Gen. 16:1)? When God wants to do something out of the ordinary, He often chooses the least likely candidate so He can get the greater glory.

This was the case with Abraham and Sarah. It seemed impossible for them to have a child. But God restated His promise. He took Abraham outside and said, "Now look toward the heavens, and count the stars, if you are able to count them. . . . So shall your descendants

be" (Gen. 15:5). At that point, Abraham believed God and was justi-
fied by his faith.

Then Abraham asked God, "O Lord GOD, how may I know that
I will possess it?" (v. 8). God's answer was the covenant ratification
ceremony we read about in the rest of Genesis 15.

God instructed Abraham to bring certain animals and prepare
them for the ceremony by cutting them in half and laying the two
sides on the ground opposite each other (vv. 9–10). Abraham prepared everything and then sat down to wait for God to show up for
the ceremony.

But as time passed, Abraham fell into a deep sleep (v. 12). God
was preparing Abraham for the ratification ceremony, but Abraham
would not be part of the process except as a witness to the event.

With Abraham watching and listening, God gave him a prophetic
summary of Israel's future bondage in Egypt and deliverance in the
Exodus under Moses, and also of Abraham's future (Gen. 15:13–16).
And then God did something very important.

> It came about when the sun had set, that it was very dark, and
> behold, there appeared a smoking oven and a flaming torch
> which passed between these pieces. On that day the LORD
> made a covenant with Abram, saying, "To your descendants
> I have given this land, from the river of Egypt as far as the
> great river, the river Euphrates" (vv. 17–18).

A Unilateral Agreement

We call this manifestation of God the *shekinah*, the glory of God,
His visible presence. God passed between the pieces of the animals
by Himself, not with Abraham, as the act of covenant ratification.

Normally, when two parties cut animals in half to make a blood
covenant, both parties walked between the pieces to seal their pledge
to keep the covenant. But God did something unique here. He took

the walk between the animals by Himself, signifying that this covenant would be totally dependent upon Him, not upon Abraham. God was saying, "Abraham, I'm going to fulfill this covenant through you and with you. But this is My covenant, and I am going to fulfill it without any conditions. I am going to do this by Myself."

The Abrahamic covenant was unconditional. God made the agreement unilaterally. Abraham was a party to the covenant, but its fulfillment was not dependent upon his keeping up his end of the agreement. That's different from the Mosaic covenant, the Law at Sinai, which was conditional upon the people's obedience and faithfulness to God.

God promised to fulfill His covenant of an heir and a land for Abraham. But as we know from the following chapters, Abraham and Sarah decided to try to help God by producing a son through Sarah's maid Hagar. The child born was named Ishmael. Of course, Ishmael's birth was very important for Bible prophecy because he became the father of the Arabs, who are still fighting with the modern nation of Israel today. As we are seeing even in our day, the Arab nations will play a role in the final unfolding of God's prophetic plan.

Why did God make His covenant with Abraham unconditional and unilateral, dependent solely upon Him for its fulfillment? Because it was a matter of honor to God. He was going to do everything He said to bring honor and glory to His name. He was going to take an old man and a barren woman and from them bring forth a nation that, although least among the nations, would put even great nations to flight.

Israel is still standing as a nation today even though her neighbors promised to drive it into the sea when the modern state of Israel was founded in 1948. Here are a few million people surrounded by many millions of their enemies, and yet Israel's enemies can't undo Israel as a nation. How can this be? The only explanation is God's faithfulness to the covenant He made with Abraham, in which He promised to bless those who blessed Abraham and curse those who cursed him.

THE LAND CONFLICT

Since we are talking about the land of Israel in relation to God's promises and prophetic program, I want to step ahead in the biblical text and look at a covenant that was made later in Israel's history as the children of Israel were on their way from Egypt to Canaan under Moses (Deut. 29–30). This is a conditional covenant often referred to as the "Palestinian covenant," or the "Land covenant." (The Bible never used the term "Palestine.")

A discussion of this covenant fits well here because we have just seen how God repeatedly promised this specific land to Abraham and his descendants forever, unconditionally.

Yet we also know that centuries later, both the northern kingdom of Israel and the southern kingdom of Judah were driven into exile from the land. And in AD 70, the Romans sacked Jerusalem, and Israel ceased to be a nation until 1948. How does all this fit together?

The Condition of Obedience

The fact that the Abrahamic covenant was unconditional did not mean that Abraham himself, or the people of Israel, had no responsibility to God. His people cannot simply live any way they want and expect to bask in His blessings with no consequences. When it comes to both the Mosaic and the Land covenants, blessing is conditioned on obedience.

We can see this element in the Land covenant. It's clear that this agreement is separate from the Mosaic covenant because the text clearly says, "These are the words of the covenant which the LORD commanded Moses to make with the sons of Israel in the land of Moab, *besides* the covenant which He had made with them at Horeb" (Deut. 29:1, italics added).

It's plain from Deuteronomy 29–30 that this covenant is conditional all the way. Obey God, and dwell in peace and safety and prosperity in the land of Israel. Disobey God, and suffer His judgment.

When He had finished announcing the covenant provisions, God put the choice squarely to Israel. "I have set before you life and death, the blessing and the curse. So choose life in order that you may live, you and your descendants" (Deut. 30:19).

Notice God didn't say anything about breaking His oath to Abraham and removing Israel from the land permanently. In fact, the only way to explain the rebirth of Israel today is God's faithfulness to His promise to Abraham. The people of Israel have not, by and large, accepted Jesus as their Messiah, so biblically speaking they are not returning to the land in obedience. But God is bringing them back in preparation for the culmination of His prophetic plan, which includes their eventual acceptance of Jesus as their Messiah (Ezek. 39:25–29; Zech. 12:10).

So God promised Israel that the land would be theirs forever. But the possession and enjoyment of the land was based on their obedience to Him. God promised the people that even though they left Him, if they would repent, He would bring them back to the land.

That's the idea behind the promise of 2 Chronicles 7:14, when God said, "[If] My people who are called by My name humble themselves and pray and seek My face and turn from their wicked ways, then I will hear from heaven, will forgive their sin and will heal their land." Restoration to the land after a period of sin was what Nehemiah was praying for as a captive in Persia (Neh. 1:4–11). When Jesus came announcing to Israel that the kingdom of God was at hand, the Jews thought they understood all that that meant. They were under Roman tyranny, but they believed that when the Messiah appeared, He would establish His kingdom and Israel would be liberated.

Jesus' offer of the kingdom to Israel did include liberation—but His primary emphasis was on the nation's spiritual condition. Israel could only receive the kingdom if the nation was repentant and willing to accept Him as Messiah. But Israel rejected Christ, and the nation was eventually driven from the land by the Romans.

Israel's Dry Bones

In Ezekiel 37:1–14, we have one of the most powerful and stark prophecies in all the Bible: the prophet's vision of the valley of dry bones. We don't have the space to quote all of these verses here. If you are familiar with the prophecy, you know that Ezekiel was puzzled by the vision. But God gave him the answer:

> Then He said to me, "Son of man, these bones are the whole house of Israel; behold, they say, 'Our bones are dried up and our hope has perished. We are completely cut off.' Therefore prophesy and say to them, 'Thus says the Lord GOD, "Behold, I will open your graves and cause you to come up out of your graves, My people; and I will bring you into the land of Israel. Then you will know that I am the LORD, when I have opened your graves and caused you to come up out of your graves, My people. I will put My Spirit within you and you will come to life, and I will place you on your own land. Then you will know that I, the LORD, have spoken and done it," declares the LORD.'" (vv. 11–14)

What a prophecy! God would take a land full of dead, dry bones and form them into a nation. This would be impossible, humanly speaking, but in May 1948 the impossible occurred. After being scattered among the other nations since AD 70, Israel became a nation again. This has never happened before or since in human history—but then no other nation is the subject of biblical prophecy the way Israel is.

Now Israel's Arab neighbors also claim the land as theirs, and this is where the battle is today. The struggle in the Middle East today turns on the fundamental question of who owns the land. You see this play out in the battles and wars taking place between Israel and her neighbors.

But there's no question in God's mind. The collection of dry bones that was Israel has been given life again, and Israel is once again in possession of at least part of its land.

THE COVENANT WITH MOSES

The Mosaic covenant, the Law given at Mount Sinai, was another conditional covenant between God and His people.

We don't need to spend a lot of time on this covenant except to note its conditional nature, and also to recall its prophetic significance in that the entire sacrificial system of the Law was designed to point to Jesus, the Lamb of God who was the full and final sacrifice for sin.

The ratification of God's covenant with Moses shows its conditional nature. The ratification ceremony is described in Exodus 24:1–8. We need to note two verses here. "Moses came and recounted to the people all the words of the LORD and all the ordinances; and all the people answered with one voice and said, 'All the words which the LORD has spoken we will do!'" (v. 3). Again in verse 7 we read, "[Moses] took the book of the covenant and read it in the hearing of the people; and they said, 'All that the LORD has spoken we will do, and we will be obedient!'"

Deuteronomy 28 also speaks to the conditional nature of the Mosaic covenant, emphasizing that its blessings were conditioned on obedience, whereas curses and judgment awaited the people if they disobeyed. It's interesting that the blessings run from verses 1–14 of this chapter, while the warnings about the curses stretch from verses 15–68. There's a lesson there about our human tendency to stray and disobey.

The bottom line of God's covenant with Moses was that if the people of Israel obeyed Him, He would bless them, and they would prosper in the land He had promised to give them. But if they disobeyed God, He would remove them from the land and disperse them among the nations.

THE COVENANT WITH DAVID

Another biblical covenant is crucial for the unfolding of prophecy. This is the Davidic covenant relating to the kingdom and the throne of Israel. God made a promise to David in 2 Samuel 7 concerning the continuation of his dynasty. Verses 1–11 were something of a prelude to the covenant, in which David expressed a desire to build a temple for God and God reviewed His faithfulness to David. Then God said:

> When your days are complete and you lie down with your fathers, I will raise up your descendant after you, who will come forth from you, and I will establish his kingdom. He shall build a house for My name, and I will establish the throne of his kingdom forever. I will be a father to him and he will be a son to Me; when he commits iniquity, I will correct him with the rod of men and the strokes of the sons of men, but My lovingkindness shall not depart from him, as I took it away from Saul, whom I removed from before you. Your house and your kingdom shall endure before Me forever; your throne shall be established forever. (vv. 12–16)

God said He was going to establish Israel, a nation that will last forever, and give this nation a land that will be theirs forever. Then He promised to establish a kingdom that will last forever. The immediate reference in the verses above is to Solomon, David's descendant. But the ultimate Ruler who will sit on David's throne forever and fulfill the Davidic covenant is the Messiah.

Jesus' Legal Claim to the Throne

This means that for Jesus' claim to be the Messiah to be valid, He had to establish two ideas: 1) He had the legal right to rule, and 2) He was, in His humanity, an ancestor of David. These ideas are established in two parts of the New Testament that some people skip over, the genealogies of Jesus in Matthew 1:1–17 and Luke 3:23–38.

Notice that in Matthew 1:1 Jesus is called "the son of David, the son of Abraham." Why do you suppose Matthew mentioned David and Abraham? Because of the Abrahamic and Davidic covenants, the two key covenants related to the land, the nation, and the throne of Israel.

We said earlier that for Jesus to qualify as Messiah to sit on David's throne, He had to establish both a legal and a birth connection to David. Matthew's genealogy links Jesus to David (see v. 6) through Joseph, who was Jesus' legal father but not His birth father, because Jesus was born of a virgin.

Therefore, Matthew demonstrated that by virtue of His adoption by Joseph, Jesus Christ has a legal right to sit on the throne of David in fulfillment of God's covenant with David.

Jesus' Birth Claim to the Throne

The genealogy in Luke traced Jesus' link to David not through Joseph's line, but through Mary's. This proved that Jesus was a descendant of David through birth since Jesus was born of Mary.

This means that Joseph and Mary did not come together by chance. Talk about a match made in heaven. When these two young righteous Jews were betrothed, it was the hand of God bringing together the two lines of David—the legal line through Joseph and the birth line through Mary. And Jesus needed both of these to validate His messianic claims.

The balance is beautiful here. Jesus would not have been qualified to be King if He were simply Mary's son. That's because Mary's own ancestry was not through Solomon, but through Solomon's brother Nathan (Luke 3:31).

In other words, Mary was a descendant of David by birth, but her particular line was not the line to which God attached the covenant promise. That promise came only through Solomon's line (1 Chron. 22:9–10).

Joseph *was* a descendant of Solomon (see Matt. 1:6), so he covered that requirement. So if either Joseph or Mary had married somebody else, Jesus wouldn't have been qualified. But He *is* qualified, and when we come to the book of Revelation, we will see Jesus taking His rightful place on David's throne as Israel's Messiah.

THE NEW COVENANT

The final covenant we need to review is the new covenant, first mentioned in Jeremiah 31. This agreement deals with the reestablishment of God's relationship with His people Israel. From Israel's standpoint, the provisions of this covenant are still future, being fulfilled when Jesus returns.

In Jeremiah 31, God told His covenant people that someday His relationship with them would be different:

> "Behold, days are coming," declares the LORD, "when I will make a new covenant with the house of Israel and with the house of Judah, not like the covenant which I made with their fathers in the day I took them by the hand to bring them out of the land of Egypt, My covenant which they broke, although I was a husband to them," declares the LORD. "But this is the covenant which I will make with the house of Israel after those days," declares the LORD. "I will put My law within them and on their heart I will write it; and I will be their God, and they shall be My people. They will not teach again, each man

his neighbor and each man his brother, saying, 'Know the LORD,' for they will all know Me, from the least of them to the greatest of them," declares the LORD, "for I will forgive their iniquity, and their sin I will remember no more." (vv. 31–34)

The former covenant God spoke of here was the covenant of Moses, the Law, which was conditional on Israel's obedience. Israel failed to keep its end of the agreement, and God brought down the curses of the covenant on His people.

But in the future, God is going to establish a new relationship with Israel that will be so rich and so dynamic the nation won't need to have His law written on stone tablets. It will be inscribed on their hearts.

Remember, the problem with the Mosaic Law wasn't the Law itself but the condition of the people's hearts. The Law of Moses revealed God's holy will and showed the people their need of regeneration.

When a person isn't right with God internally, no external statute can give that person a right relationship with God. But when a person loves God with all his heart, he is enabled to fulfill the demands of God's law because his motivation is to please and obey God, and because God has replaced his old heart with a new one (Ezek. 11:19; 36:26). This is the new covenant.

The church partakes of the benefits of the new covenant. On the night of His betrayal, at the Last Supper, Jesus gave the cup to His disciples and said, "This cup which is poured out for you is the new covenant in My blood" (Luke 22:20). We are told to partake of this cup and the bread as part of the new covenant Jesus instituted in His death (1 Cor. 11:25–26). The new covenant is lived from the inside out, not from the outside in like the Law of Moses. We as believers today are living under the new covenant—and the day is coming when the people of Israel will also follow their Messiah, Jesus Christ, with all their hearts when He comes to reign on David's throne in His millennial kingdom.

5

PROPHECY AND ISRAEL'S TIMETABLE

If you have ever streamed a track meet online or attended one personally, you know that these events often look chaotic. You may see some athletes practicing their high jump or pole vault, while others run or stretch on the infield, all while a row of runners is lining up on the track for another event.

Large numbers of people seem to be meandering around with no one clearly in charge. But the chaos is only apparent, because officials and timekeepers are firmly in control of every aspect of the meet. When it's time for a race or a field event, that area is cleared, and the competitors move to their places to get ready. In the midst of apparent chaos, the officials are in firm control.

Our world often looks like a track meet. Life can seem chaotic, out of control. At times like this, we may wonder where God is. But we who know God and His Word understand that He is in charge even when that doesn't seem to be the case. And when God blows the whistle to signal the start of an event, everything comes together according to the purpose of His own will.

Prophecy gives us a perfect example of God's perfect control over the events of people and nations—and nowhere is His sovereign control clearer in prophecy than in the series of events known as Daniel's seventy weeks.

This prophecy of Israel's timetable is found in Daniel 9:24–27, where we are going to spend the bulk of this chapter. We'll also look at several other passages that relate to Daniel 9, since this passage is what we might call a hub in the prophetic wheel.

Almost all of this great prophecy has been fulfilled from our perspective today, but the one "week" that is still future takes us right to the heart of the end times in the book of Revelation. There is a lot of good stuff here, so let's start unpacking it.

BACKGROUND TO THE PROPHECY

Before we plunge into the details of Israel's seventy weeks, we need to see this prophecy in its context in Daniel 9. Verse 1 indicates that this prophecy was given to Daniel many years after the prophecies of Gentile domination in chapters 4 and 7.

Daniel's Discovery

Daniel was an elderly man at this time. He had been in exile for about sixty-seven years—a number that's very important, as we will see below. He was now serving in the court of Darius, king of the Medo-Persian Empire.

Daniel recorded that in the first year of Darius's reign, he "observed in the books the number of the years which was revealed as the word of the LORD to Jeremiah the prophet for the completion of the desolations of Jerusalem, namely, seventy years" (Dan. 9:2). In other words, Daniel was having his devotions one day when he read something in the prophecy of Jeremiah that apparently startled him. Daniel was probably reading Jeremiah 25:11–12:

"This whole land will be a desolation and a horror, and these nations will serve the king of Babylon seventy years.

Then it will be when seventy years are completed I will punish the king of Babylon and that nation," declares the LORD, "for their iniquity, and the land of the Chaldeans; and I will make it an everlasting desolation."

Later Jeremiah recorded this promise from the Lord: "For thus says the LORD, 'When seventy years have been completed for Babylon, I will visit you and fulfill My good word to you, to bring you back to this place'" (29:10). Daniel was almost certainly aware of this prophecy too.

Here's what jumped off the page to Daniel. He was reading this in 538 BC, sixty-seven years after Nebuchadnezzar had come to Jerusalem in 605 BC and taken Daniel and other Israelites as captives to Babylon. God said through Jeremiah that Israel's captivity would last seventy years—so, due to understanding the nature of prophecy and God's Word, Daniel realized that Israel's captivity was about to end.

Daniel's Repentance

The first thing Daniel did after reading Jeremiah was not run out and tell his fellow Israelite exiles to put their Babylonian real estate on the market and start packing.

Instead, Daniel immediately fell on his face and poured out his heart to God in an incredible prayer of confession and repentance on behalf of his nation Israel (Dan. 9:3–19). In this prayer, Daniel personally identified with the sins of Israel more than thirty times. Why did Daniel do this? Because he knew the Law of Moses, including the blessings God had promised Israel for obedience and the curses He had pronounced against them if they disobeyed.

We looked at these earlier in Deuteronomy 28, noting that the curse for disobedience included banishment from the land of Israel.

I'm convinced Daniel also knew God's promise that if Israel in her exile would return to Him in repentance, He would bring the people back to their land (Deut. 30:1–4).

It's obvious from the way Daniel prayed that he knew the Law: "Indeed all Israel has transgressed Your law and turned aside, not obeying Your voice; so the curse has been poured out on us, along with the oath which is written in the law of Moses the servant of God, for we have sinned against Him" (Dan. 9:11).

Israel's Sin

Before we go any further in Daniel, what was Israel's particular sin that brought the judgment of God upon the nation in the form of the seventy-year Babylonian captivity? The answer is also in the Mosaic Law, having to do with the land itself:

> Speak to the sons of Israel and say to them, "When you come into the land which I shall give you, then the land shall have a sabbath to the LORD. Six years you shall sow your field, and six years you shall prune your vineyard and gather in its crop, but during the seventh year the land shall have a sabbath rest, a sabbath to the LORD; you shall not sow your field nor prune your vineyard." (Lev. 25:2–4)

This command to let the land of Israel rest every seventh year goes back to creation, when God rested on the seventh day and sanctified it. Sabbath observance was later made a part of Moses' Law (Ex. 20:8–11).

God rested and enjoyed His creation on the seventh day, and He wanted His people to quit their work and enjoy Him every seventh day. He also wanted to teach them that He could provide for their needs quite adequately in six days. It was an issue of trusting God to provide on that seventh day.

So the people of Israel were to have a Sabbath rest every seventh day, and the land was to have a Sabbath rest every seventh year. During that year, the people were not to plant or harvest any crops, but trust God to provide for them.

It would take faith on the Israelites' part to believe that God would give them enough food to last them all of that seventh year if they obeyed Him and quit farming after six years. But that is exactly what God wanted from His people: their faith in Him and obedience to His commands.

God also added a warning of what would happen if Israel failed to observe its Sabbath years and let the land lie fallow:

> I will scatter [you] among the nations and will draw out a sword after you, as your land becomes desolate and your cities become waste.
>
> Then the land will enjoy its sabbaths all the days of the desolation, while you are in your enemies' land; then the land will rest and enjoy its sabbaths. All the days of its desolation it will observe the rest which it did not observe on your sabbaths, while you were living on it. (Lev. 26:33–35)

Because the nation did in fact fail to observe the Sabbath year, this warning became a prophecy of future captivity. The northern kingdom of Israel was taken by Assyria, and the southern kingdom of Judah was conquered and enslaved by Babylon under Nebuchadnezzar.

In other words, the Israelites were working the land all seven years instead of trusting God, so He removed them from the land. This brings us back full circle to the book of Daniel, where the Israelites were actually living out the punishment described hundreds of years earlier in the Law and later prophesied in the book of Jeremiah.

Israel's Exile

Apparently, the exile was for seventy years because Israel had failed to observe seventy Sabbath years. The language of the curse suggests that Israel would be in exile until the land received all the rest it had missed during their years of disobedience. So God decreed one year of exile for each Sabbath year missed. Remember, the promise of restoration in Deuteronomy 30:1–4 was conditioned on the nation's repentance.

Now we know why Daniel fell on his face and prayed the way he did. He realized that even though God had given His people a prophetic timetable for their return to Israel, that timetable would not be actualized apart from repentance. Daniel offered a tremendous prayer of repentance on behalf of his nation.

THE PROPHECY REVEALED TO DANIEL

Now we're ready for the next link in this chain. It was while Daniel was praying that God sent the angel Gabriel to him with the prophecy of the seventy weeks.

It's not recorded in Daniel's prayer that he asked God to show him what was next on Israel's agenda after the Babylonian captivity was over. But that would be a natural question on Daniel's mind, and perhaps he was wondering what God was going to do with His people.

The Prophecy's Duration

This is the question that Gabriel was sent to answer (Dan. 9:20–24). The angel told Daniel, "I have now come forth to give you insight with understanding . . . so give heed to the message and gain understanding of the vision" (vv. 22–23).

What follows in verses 24–27 is the prophecy called the seventy weeks, literally "seventy sevens." The idea is not seventy units of seven days each, but seventy units of seven *years* each. This fits the context, because Daniel had just been reading in Jeremiah about the seventy years of captivity. Also, the prophecy covers far too much time to be anything but seventy units of seven years, or a total of 490 years.

The prophecy begins, "Seventy weeks have been decreed for your people and your holy city, to finish the transgression, to make an end of sin, to make atonement for iniquity, to bring in everlasting righteousness, to seal up vision and prophecy and to anoint the most holy place" (Dan. 9:24).

The Prophecy's Specifics

Gabriel gave Daniel six specific things that would be accomplished during the period of the seventy weeks. This 490-year period would "finish the transgression," a reference to ending Israel's rebellion and bringing her to repentance. God would also "make an end of sin," imparting to the Israelites new spiritual life through the new covenant.

Gabriel also said the seventy weeks would "make atonement for iniquity," pointing forward to the death of Christ as the final atonement offered for Israel's sin. The fourth item on the list is "to bring in everlasting righteousness" (Dan. 9:24). This is a reference to Christ's millennial kingdom when He will rule in righteousness and the righteous will rule with Him (Jer. 23:5–6).

The final two items on the angel's list are "to seal up vision and prophecy," to fulfill all the prophecies concerning Israel, and to "anoint the most holy place." Since the word *place* is not in the original, I take it Gabriel is referring to the anointing of the Messiah.

The Prophecy's Starting Point

That's the panorama of the entire period. Then the angel revealed to Daniel how the seventy weeks would unfold. "So you are to know and discern that from the issuing of a decree to restore and rebuild Jerusalem until Messiah the Prince there will be seven weeks and sixty-two weeks; it will be built again, with plaza and moat, even in times of distress" (Dan. 9:25).

The angel said that God's prophetic clock would start ticking on this period of seventy weeks when a decree was issued to rebuild Jerusalem. From that moment until the appearance of the Messiah would be seven plus sixty-two weeks, which in the formula of the weeks is 483 years. Keep that figure in mind.

The decree referred to in Daniel 9 would not be issued until more than one hundred years after Daniel, in 444 BC by the Persian king Artaxerxes. The decree came about because of the burden for Jerusalem and the mighty prayer of Nehemiah, a Jewish exile and the king's trusted servant (Neh. 1:1–11).

You probably know the story. Artaxerxes noticed Nehemiah's distress and asked him what was wrong. When Nehemiah explained his agony over the desolate condition of Jerusalem, Artaxerxes sent him back to Jerusalem with permission to rebuild the city and gave him official letters to acquire what he needed. This was the decree referred to in Daniel 9:25.

Nehemiah 2:1 pinpoints the date for us on this decree because he said it came in the twentieth year of Artaxerxes' reign. So we can establish the date as 444 BC. That's when the clock started counting down on Daniel's seventy weeks.

Some Jews in exile had gone back to Jerusalem prior to this time, but from the standpoint of Israel's prophetic timetable it was the decree of Artaxerxes that got the clock moving. Within the first seven weeks of Daniel's prophecy, or forty-nine years, the city was rebuilt "even in times of distress" (Dan. 9:25). Nehemiah experienced some of those times in Jerusalem himself as his enemies first taunted him and then tried to kill him.

The Prophecy's Messiah

The next distinct segment in the seventy weeks is the sixty-two weeks from the time of Jerusalem's restoration until the appearance of the Messiah. Altogether, then, the angel said we are to count off sixty-nine weeks, or 483 years, from the decree concerning Jerusalem to the Messiah.

Now we're ready for Daniel 9:26, the next piece of the prophecy. "Then after the sixty-two weeks the Messiah will be cut off and have nothing, and the people of the prince who is to come will destroy the city and the sanctuary. And its end will come with a flood; even to the end there will be war; desolations are determined."

This is where we see a clear break between the end of the sixty-ninth week and the beginning of the seventieth week. Messiah's cutting off was a prophecy of Jesus Christ's death on the cross, after which Jerusalem would suffer another destruction by a different people.

The "prince who is to come" is a reference to the Antichrist, the final world ruler who will reign over a restored Roman Empire. This is the "little horn" (Dan. 7:8) who seizes world power. Therefore, the "people of the prince" has to refer to the Romans, who did in fact come against Jerusalem and so completely destroy the city and the temple in AD 70 that there wasn't even one stone left on another, as Jesus Himself prophesied (see Matt. 24:2).

That's the basic scenario of what happened at the end of the first sixty-nine weeks of Daniel's prophecy. Let's see how accurate this prophecy is, since Daniel was writing more than five hundred years before the fact.

The Prophecy's Accuracy

The key to plugging Daniel's prophecy into history is to know that he was writing about prophetic years, which are different from our calendar years. Whenever the Bible speaks of prophecy it measures time in prophetic years, which are thirty days a month for twelve months, for a total of 360 days a year. This concept of the 360-day prophetic year is arrived at by comparing the last half of Daniel's seventieth week (Dan. 9:27b), which is three-and-a-half years, with the 1,260 days of Revelation 11:3 and 12:6 and the forty-two months of

Revelation 11:2 and 13:5. The number of days works out to thirty days a month, or 360 days a year. Using this figure of 360 days per year, multiplied by the 483 years of Daniel's first sixty-nine weeks, gives us a total of 173,880 days. This is the length of time from the decree to rebuild Jerusalem in 444 BC to the Messiah being cut off.

Many Bible students have done the calculations, which show that this length of time brings us from 444 BC to March AD 33, the month in which Jesus was crucified. You can either call this an incredible coincidence or sheer good luck, or you can say God has the whole world in His hands! Like the official at the track meet, He has all the seeming chaos of world events firmly under His control.

So at the end of the sixty-ninth week as prophesied in Daniel 9:26, the Messiah was cut off. Jesus was crucified, and He had nothing. He was a King, but He had no earthly kingdom.

After Christ's death, the clock stopped ticking on Daniel's prophecy. The nation of Israel entered a time of parenthesis that continues until this day, and will continue until the tribulation, a seven-year period that will constitute Daniel's seventieth week.

Just before His crucifixion, Jesus said, "Jerusalem, Jerusalem, who kills the prophets and stones those who are sent to her! How often I wanted to gather your children together, the way a hen gathers her chicks under her wings, and you were unwilling. Behold, your house is being left to you desolate!" (Matt. 23:37–38).

Then in Matthew 24:2, Jesus prophesied the destruction of Jerusalem and the temple that occurred in AD 70 under the Roman general Titus. Speaking of the temple, Jesus said, "Do you not see all these things? Truly I say to you, not one stone here will be left upon another, which will not be torn down."

This was history before it was written because that's exactly what happened. Jesus even prophesied that Jerusalem would be trampled by Gentiles, the Romans (Luke 21:24). When the temple was destroyed in AD 70 by the Romans, the Jews lost all their genealogical records of the twelve tribes, since those records were stored in the temple. To this day, the Jews do not know their tribal descent because all those records went up in smoke when the Romans sacked the temple.

But God preserved one genealogy, the record of Jesus Christ. That's why we have the genealogy of Christ in Matthew and Luke. It was necessary to have this record to prove that Jesus was the Messiah. This is all part of God's prophetic program.

The Prophecy's Gap

One series of sevens, the seventieth week, stands out as distinct in the prophecy of Daniel 9. The prophet marks a clear division between the first sixty-nine weeks and the seventieth week, but what Daniel didn't reveal is the nature or the length of the gap separating the sixty-ninth and seventieth weeks. We have to turn to the New Testament for that information.

When Jesus told His disciples, "I will build My church" (Matt. 16:18), He was announcing the start of a new program in God's plan of the ages. What we learn is that the final week of Israel's prophetic program was being put on hold. The clock has stopped for Israel, and God's primary focus will now be upon the building of a new entity called the church.

The church is different from national Israel because the church is made up of Jews and Gentiles, coming together to form one new body called the body of Christ (Eph. 2:11–22). God hasn't ceased His program with Israel, but because Israel did not repent and receive its Messiah, the nation was put on the sidelines, prophetically speaking.

God called a "timeout" on Israel for a period of time called the "church age." So far, that timeout has lasted for nearly two thousand years, and it continues for Israel today.

DANIEL'S SEVENTIETH WEEK

Now let's go back to Daniel 9 and finish the prophecy of the seventy weeks:

> And he will make a firm covenant with the many for one week, but in the middle of the week he will put a stop to sacrifice and grain offering; and on the wing of abominations will come one who makes desolate, even until a complete destruction, one that is decreed, is poured out on the one who makes desolate. (v. 27)

The Israelites were restored to their land after the captivity, but the people did not really repent. Jesus Christ came preaching this message: "Repent, for the kingdom of heaven is at hand" (Matt. 4:17). But instead of receiving their Messiah, the nation rejected Him and cut Him off. They put Christ to death on the cross. The crucifixion marked the end of Daniel's sixty-ninth week and stopped the clock on Israel's prophetic program.

Starting the Clock Again

That clock will start ticking again during the seven-year period known as the tribulation, as I said above. During this yet-future period, God will complete His program with Israel to bring the nation to repentance, cleanse her of her sin, fulfill His promises, and accomplish all the other things the angel outlined in Daniel 9:24.

When you go to Israel today, as I have done, it becomes obvious that God has not yet finished working with His chosen people. The temple is still gone, with only the famous Western Wall standing. Rabbis and others go there to pray for the Messiah to come and to weep because the temple is destroyed, and they can't offer sacrifices.

Christ is the final sacrifice; there is no further need for blood sacrifices, but unbelieving Jews reject Christ's sacrifice. From their standpoint, the reason they can't rebuild their temple is that there is a Muslim mosque sitting on the Temple Mount, the site where they believe the Jewish temple once stood. Israel could not touch that mosque without setting off a potential global war, but without a temple they can't offer sacrifices.

Traditional Jewish worship has been unraveled since AD 70 when the Romans destroyed the temple. If you ask an orthodox Jew what they are waiting for, they will tell you, "We are waiting for the Messiah." The problem is not that orthodox, or even conservative, Jews don't believe the Old Testament. It's that they reject Jesus as Messiah.

The Antichrist's Covenant

So Israel is out of the spotlight in God's program until Daniel's seventieth week. This week will begin when he "make[s] a firm covenant with the many for one week" (Dan. 9:27), that is, for seven years.

The person making this covenant is the "prince who is to come" (Dan. 9:26). We saw above that this is the Antichrist making a covenant of peace with Israel, which he will break after three-and-a-half years. This is the tribulation, when God resumes His program with Israel. The church will not be part of this painful period because we will be raptured before the tribulation begins, further proof that the church is distinct from Israel in God's plan (Rev. 3:10).

The Antichrist is going to rise to the top in Europe, which is the remnants of the old Roman Empire, and he is going to make a peace plan that will seem to bring permanent peace to Israel and the Middle East.

Breaking the Covenant

But according to Daniel 9:27, this leader will break the covenant at the halfway point. In Revelation 11:1, the apostle John was told to measure the temple of God in Jerusalem. This is the temple that apparently will be built during the tribulation period. The Jews will again be offering sacrifices during the first half of this seven-year period.

But when the Antichrist breaks his covenant, Daniel says the sacrifices will stop. Daniel's prophecy anticipates the temple John saw in his vision because the Bible is perfectly consistent with itself.

John was told to measure the temple, but not the "court," which is the court of the Gentiles. Why was John told not to measure this part? Because "it has been given to the nations; and they will tread under foot the holy city for forty-two months" (Rev. 11:2). That's three-and-a-half years, the second half of Israel's seventieth week.

When the Antichrist first comes on the scene, everybody is going to be excited because, finally, there will be peace in the Middle East. But halfway through the covenant Antichrist is going to reveal himself for who he really is.

His real identity is terrible because Daniel 9:27 says he will come "on the wing of abominations." The Antichrist will set himself up as God in Israel's temple. And anyone who doesn't acknowledge and worship him by having the number 666, the mark of the Beast, imprinted on his forehead or right hand will be subject to persecution and death. The only reason people would refuse that number is because they believe in Jesus Christ.

The last half of Daniel's seventieth week is going to be hell on earth. John said of the Antichrist, also called the Beast:

There was given to him a mouth speaking arrogant words and blasphemies, and authority to act for forty-two months was given to him. And he opened his mouth in blasphemies against God, to blaspheme His name and His tabernacle, that is, those who dwell in heaven.

It was also given to him to make war with the saints and to overcome them, and authority over every tribe and people and tongue and nation was given to him. All who dwell on the

earth will worship him, everyone whose name has not been
written from the foundation of the world in the book of life
of the Lamb who has been slain. (Rev. 13:5–8)

It's hard even to imagine the chaos and terrible things that are
going to be unleashed on earth when the Antichrist reveals himself
and turns his wrath on Israel and the saints of God.

GOD IS IN CONTROL

But if Daniel's prophecy of the seventy weeks tells us anything, it's
that God has this whole thing under control. His prophetic program
is timed so exactly that He can pinpoint the arrival of Jesus Christ
and His crucifixion down to the day.

What does all of this have to do with our lives today? Everything!
It means we can trust what God says even when we don't know all the
details. Whether it's our daily Christian lives or the plan of the ages,
God is going to bring His will to pass.

How is He going to do it? I don't know. When is He going to do
it? I don't know. But I know He is God, and we can trust Him for the
details.

God controls everything. Even the devil, through the Antichrist,
will only do what he is permitted to do because, beneath the seeming chaos of world events, God is running this show. The One who
established and orchestrated Israel's 490-year plan has the timetable
of your life in His hands. And He is always right on time.

6

PROPHECY AND THE CHURCH AGE

When I was in college, and later in seminary, the professor usually handed out a course syllabus on the first day of a new class. The syllabus was an outline of the course, with enough detail to let me know what the professor expected of me and where the course was going. The syllabus gave the highlights of the class, but not every detail of every lecture or assignment. Those came as the class unfolded.

Another thing the syllabus did was let me and my classmates know who was in charge of the class. It was clear from the syllabus that the professor had the authority to choose the assignments and the reading we would do.

Bible prophecy is like a course syllabus. God doesn't give us every detail of His program, but He gives us enough so we can know where history is going and what He expects of us. And just as important is the fact that the Bible lets us know *whose* history this is. History is "His story." It is the outworking of God's plan for the ages. He is clearly in charge. We're about to see from the book of Daniel that

God is firmly in charge when it comes to the unfolding of His prophetic plan for the Gentiles, the other nations on earth.

GENTILE WORLD HISTORY

Daniel's prophecy deals in depth with the progress of Gentile world history, and the amazing thing is that we can verify much of Daniel's prophecy by opening our secular history books and laying recorded history alongside Daniel's prophecies written hundreds of years earlier.

That is the time we are living in. The church today is predominantly Gentile, and for the most part the Jews remain in their unbelief and rejection of Jesus Christ as their Messiah. Many Bible scholars agree that the times of the Gentiles began with the conquest and destruction of Jerusalem by the Babylonians under King Nebuchadnezzar and the deportation of the people to exile in Babylon (Dan. 1:1–7).

One of the Jewish exiles deported to Babylon was Daniel, a young teenager of exceptional character and ability. He was trained to be one of Nebuchadnezzar's court advisers, and when the king had a dream that no one could interpret, God gave the meaning to Daniel.

Daniel was a righteous young man, refusing to defile himself and break God's law even though he was a captive of the most powerful king on earth. Daniel's life was as much a witness to God's sovereign power as was his prophecy.

NEBUCHADNEZZAR'S DREAM

The prophetic portion of Daniel begins in chapter 2 with Nebuchadnezzar's dreams. This mighty king was so disturbed by this recurring dream, and so eager to know what it meant, that he called all his wise men together to interpret it for him (Dan. 2:1–3).

The problem was Nebuchadnezzar either couldn't, or wouldn't, tell these men what the dream was. But being the king, he demanded an explanation anyway, and he ordered all his counselors in Babylon to be killed when the sorcerers and magicians couldn't tell him the dream (vv. 4–15).

That death order included Daniel and his three friends—who hadn't been present when the king originally asked for an interpretation of the dream—so Daniel asked for some time. Then he and his three Hebrew friends went to prayer, and God revealed the interpretation of the dream to Daniel (Dan. 2:16–19).

Notice that "Daniel blessed the God of heaven" (v. 19) for this answer to prayer. Five times in this book, God is called "the God of heaven." Daniel went to God for wisdom on something he didn't understand, and God gave him insight. Daniel then immediately praised and thanked God for the answer.

Daniel received his answer from God and went before Nebuchadnezzar. The exchange leading up to Daniel's interpretation was a powerful testimony on his part, which you can read for yourself (Dan. 2:24–30).

Daniel told the king that he saw a great statue in his dream, a statue whose "appearance was awesome" (v. 31). Daniel described this magnificent statue as having a head made of gold, a chest and arms of silver, a belly and thighs of bronze, legs of iron, and feet made of a mixture of iron and clay.

Then Daniel said a stone "cut out without hands" struck the statue on its feet and crushed them (v. 34). After that, all of the statue was crushed, and the metals blown away completely like chaff in the wind. But "the stone that struck the statue became a great mountain and filled the whole earth" (v. 35c). Once Daniel had told Nebuchadnezzar his dream, he moved immediately to the interpretation.

Interpreting the Dream

Nebuchadnezzar himself was the head of gold because, as far as earthly powers were concerned, he was currently "the king of kings"

(Dan. 2:37). But God made it clear that Nebuchadnezzar's power wouldn't last forever. In fact, the eventual demise of the Babylonian Empire was contained in the rest of the statue. Daniel continued:

> After you there will arise another kingdom inferior to you, then another third kingdom of bronze, which will rule over all the earth.
> Then there will be a fourth kingdom as strong as iron; inasmuch as iron crushes and shatters all things, so, like iron that breaks in pieces, it will crush and break all these in pieces. (vv. 39–40)

Daniel's prophecy of the four major Gentile empires of the ancient world is so accurate that many critics claim he had to have written his book after the fact. Daniel wrote in the sixth century BC, hundreds of years before the rise of the Greek or Roman Empires. Yet his prophecy is so accurate we can verify it with a history book. The kingdom illustrated by a chest and arms of silver was the Medo-Persian Empire that overthrew Babylon many decades later, when Daniel as an old man was serving the Babylonian king Belshazzar. The Medes and the Persians defeated Babylon on the very night of Belshazzar's drunken feast (Dan. 5:20–31).

The third kingdom of bronze was the kingdom of Greece under Alexander the Great, who destroyed the Medo-Persian Empire and did in fact "rule over all the earth" (Dan. 2:39). It's obvious that when Daniel came to the fourth kingdom something was different, because it occupied more of the vision than any of the other kingdoms. This was the great Roman Empire that crushed Greece and became the most dominant empire in the ancient world. The Roman Empire ruled the known world when Jesus arrived on the scene.

But even though Rome's military might was unmatched, it had

a flaw, a weakness, that eventually brought down the empire. Daniel described this mixture:

> In that you saw the feet and toes, partly of potter's clay and partly of iron, it will be a divided kingdom; but it will have in it the toughness of iron, inasmuch as you saw the iron mixed with common clay. As the toes of the feet were partly of iron and partly of pottery, so some of the kingdom will be strong and part of it will be brittle. And in that you saw the iron mixed with common clay, they will combine with one another in the seed of men; but they will not adhere to one another, even as iron does not combine with pottery. (Dan. 2:41–43)

From God's perspective, the thing that distinguished the Roman Empire was its mixture of iron and clay, two substances that cannot stay together. In other words, the flaw in the Roman Empire could not be fixed. Something would cause this kingdom to come apart.

This prophecy was fulfilled because the Roman Empire did come apart, but not by military conquest. Rome was brought down by decay from within as immorality, wanton luxury, and unrestrained living mixed with Rome's governmental structures to weaken the kingdom's moral will and desire to rule effectively.

The fact that the mixture was in the toes and not in the legs indicates that Rome became weak in its later stages, which again is true historically. Rome became so decadent and licentious that it could not survive as a world power.

God's Kingdom

The revelation of the four great world empires is now followed by the revelation of another kingdom, the eternal kingdom of God:

And in the days of those kings the God of heaven will set up a kingdom which will never be destroyed, and that kingdom will not be left for another people; it will crush and put an end to all these kingdoms, but it will itself endure forever. Inasmuch as you saw that a stone was cut out of the mountain without hands and that it crushed the iron, the bronze, the clay, the silver and the gold, the great God has made known to the king what will take place in the future; so the dream is true and its interpretation is trustworthy. (Dan. 2:44–45)

This kingdom is yet future, being fulfilled when Jesus Christ returns to set up His millennial kingdom. He is the stone cut out without hands, which means He is from God.

Jesus is called a stone throughout Scripture (1 Peter 2:4–8), and in this dream the stone becomes a mountain, which in the Bible symbolizes a kingdom. At His return, Christ will crush all earthly powers, and His kingdom will rule over the earth.

DANIEL'S VISION

Many years after interpreting Nebuchadnezzar's dream concerning the times of the Gentiles, Daniel himself had a dream and a vision related to the same four earthly kingdoms (Dan. 7).

The interesting thing about this is the difference in perspective between the dream of a pagan king and the vision God gave His holy prophet. The sequence of the kingdoms is the same, and their eventual destruction, but what a difference in the way they are presented.

In Nebuchadnezzar's dream, these world powers were magnificent to behold in their glory, an awe-inspiring statue that was "large and of extraordinary splendor" (Dan. 2:31). But in Daniel 7, from God's perspective, these kingdoms are wild beasts, meant to be destroyed.

Their true nature as sinful, rebellious empires is revealed when God shines His light on them.

Daniel wrote, "I was looking in my vision by night, and behold, the four winds of heaven were stirring up the great sea. And four great beasts were coming up from the sea, different from one another" (Dan. 7:2–3).

The "four winds" is a reference to angelic activity, when angels address the wickedness of men (see Rev. 7:1–3). The "great sea" in the Bible is always the Mediterranean Sea, so what we have in Daniel 7, as in Revelation 7, is God addressing Gentile rulers. Daniel saw four beasts, four Gentile kingdoms in the area around the Mediterranean Sea, which was the center of the world at that time.

The First Beast

The first beast in the vision "was like a lion and had the wings of an eagle. I kept looking until its wings were plucked, and it was lifted up from the ground and made to stand on two feet like a man; a human mind also was given to it" (v. 4).

We just saw that the first great Gentile world empire addressed in prophecy is Babylon, particularly under Nebuchadnezzar. This beast was like a lion in its strength; the lion is the king of beasts. The eagle is the king of the air, so when combined with a lion the picture is one of total domination. That's what Babylon had under King Nebuchadnezzar. He was the golden head of the great statue in Daniel 2. Nebuchadnezzar ruled for more than forty years, and he ran the whole show.

But Nebuchadnezzar got into trouble when he started looking at himself as the master of the universe. Nebuchadnezzar started believing his own press clippings. Thus, according to Daniel's vision, the eagle got his wings plucked. What happens when a bird gets its wings plucked? It can no longer fly! Daniel 4:28–37 tells the story of Nebuchadnezzar's judgment by God. The king was on his rooftop, looking over the city of Babylon and boasting about his own glory. Immediately, the Bible says, God struck Nebuchadnezzar with insanity.

The king's hair started to grow long, and his fingernails grew out. He was bent down on all fours like an animal, and for seven years he lived in animal-like insanity. At the end of that time, God restored his sanity, and Nebuchadnezzar bowed to the true God. This is a sobering lesson for any of us who are tempted to develop a "theo-ego," a God complex.

God is in control. He sets up kings and He brings down kings. Listen to Nebuchadnezzar's testimony. "He is able to humble those who walk in pride" (Dan. 4:37). You and I are only what God allows us to be. Daniel's vision depicted Nebuchadnezzar getting his sanity back after seven years when he was stood back up on his feet after crawling around like a beast (Dan. 7:4).

Eventually, though, Babylon got its wings plucked by the Medo-Persian Empire. In the reign of Belshazzar, at the end of his drunken party, the Persian army under King Darius launched a surprise attack.

The Second Beast

The Medo-Persian Empire is the second beast of Daniel's vision. Of this beast the prophet wrote, "Behold, another beast, a second one, resembling a bear. And it was raised up on one side, and three ribs were in its mouth between its teeth; and thus they said to it, 'Arise, devour much meat!'" (Dan. 7:5).

Why is the bear raised on one side? Because the Persians defeated the Medes and absorbed them into the Medo-Persian Empire. Persia was the greater of the two empires, and combined they were able to defeat Babylon.

The three ribs in the bear's mouth symbolized the three great enemies that Persia defeated in its conquest: Egypt, Assyria, and Babylon. All of them were conquered by the Medo-Persian Empire, which ruled for some two hundred years.

The Third Beast

In Daniel 7:6, Daniel described the third beast of his vision, the Greek Empire established by Alexander the Great. "After this I kept looking, and behold, another one, like a leopard, which had on its back four wings of a bird; the beast also had four heads, and dominion was given to it."

A leopard is fast on its feet, so when you add that image to one of a bird with four wings instead of the normal two, you have the picture of lightning speed. The Greeks under Alexander the Great defeated the Medo-Persian Empire in a matter of a few months in 334 BC, and Alexander the Great had conquered the world by the time he was thirty years old.

The end of verse 6 is another example of the accuracy of Bible prophecy. The four heads of the Greek Empire that Daniel saw refer to the four kingdoms into which Alexander's domain was split after his death.

Alexander's four generals fought among themselves for power, and the Greek Empire was split four ways. These commanders were able to divide the kingdom because the strong leader who had held it together was gone. So eventually the Greek Empire passed off the world scene as a ruling power.

The Fourth Beast

This is where things really take off in terms of prophecy and the times of the Gentiles. The fourth beast of Daniel's vision corresponds to the fourth part of Nebuchadnezzar's statue, the Roman Empire symbolized by iron. But here God gave Daniel a much more complete picture of the progression of Gentile world domination because we find that the Roman Empire will appear in history again, except in a different form.

Daniel said of the fourth beast, "I kept looking in the night visions, and behold, a fourth beast, dreadful and terrifying and extremely strong; and it had large iron teeth. It devoured and crushed and trampled down the remainder with its feet; and it was different from all the beasts that were before it, and it had ten horns" (Dan. 7:7). This beast was horrifying to see.

The statue in Nebuchadnezzar's dream had ten toes, which were said to be kings (Dan. 2:44). Now we read about ten horns, which are also ten kings or kingdoms that were coming out of this kingdom.

Daniel said that as he was studying this terrifying image, trying to figure it out, "Behold, another horn, a little one, came up among them, and three of the first horns were pulled out by the roots before it; and behold, this horn possessed eyes like the eyes of a man and a mouth uttering great boasts" (Dan. 7:8).

Look ahead for a minute to verse 11. "Then I kept looking because of the sound of the boastful words which the horn was speaking; I kept looking until the beast was slain, and its body was destroyed and given to the burning fire."

The "little horn" of Daniel 7 is called the Beast in Revelation 13:1. This is the Antichrist, the final world ruler whose reign of terror in the tribulation will bring to a completion the times of the Gentiles, when Israel is trodden down by the nations. The Antichrist will be the worst persecutor of Israel in history.

I urge you to read the rest of Daniel 7. But let me put this great prophecy of verses 7–28 in perspective. The Roman Empire was destroyed from within, the clay mixing with the iron. The breakup of this great empire eventually resulted in the establishment of the nations that make up Europe.

Even though the old Roman Empire is gone, at some point in the future a new confederation of ten nations will arise in Europe, constituting a revived Roman Empire. These are the ten horns of Daniel's prophecy.

Notice that the little horn, the Antichrist, had eyes and a mouth making great boasts. This is a human being. The eyes have to do with his intelligence. This is a brilliant person, the epitome of an ungodly ruler who will make all the tyrants and dictators of history look like schoolchildren.

This ruler, energized and controlled by Satan as his counterfeit Christ, will step into this ten-nation kingdom and conquer three of the nations, pulling them up by the roots. The Antichrist will take control and become the ruler of the world, although his power won't be obvious at first because he begins as a "little horn" among other horns. The Antichrist will blaspheme God and "wear down the saints of the Highest One" (Dan. 7:25). He will also make claims to deity and persecute Israel horribly.

God in Control

There are two other persons in Daniel 7 we haven't mentioned yet: the Ancient of Days (vv. 9–10), and the Son of Man (vv. 13–14). These are God the Father and God the Son. The story isn't over, and Daniel's vision of Gentile world powers isn't complete, until these two have acted.

In verse 9, Daniel wrote, "I kept looking until thrones were set up, and the Ancient of Days took His seat." Don't worry about the Antichrist, because God is taking His seat to pronounce judgment and bring a swift end to this satanically inspired impostor.

God is called the Ancient of Days here because He's the timeless One. He takes His throne while all of this chaos is happening on earth. The scene Daniel was shown is the great tribulation, when the Antichrist will have his way with the world for three-and-a-half years. But just as things get to their worst, the Ancient of Days takes His throne. God is still in control.

Then Daniel saw "One like a Son of Man" coming up to the Ancient of Days, God the Father (Dan. 7:13). The Father presents this Son of Man with an everlasting kingdom that cannot be destroyed (v. 14). This is a prophetic picture of God the Father handing over to His

Son, the Lord Jesus Christ, the kingdoms of this world for Him to rule.

Jesus often called Himself "the Son of Man" in the New Testament (Matt. 24:30; 26:64). He was born of a woman, so He is the Son of Man, the One to fulfill the promise of Genesis 3:15 that God would use a Man, the seed of the woman, to bring the earth under His dominion (Rev. 20:1–6; Ps. 2:6–9; 1 Cor. 15:24–25).

The end of Daniel's vision reveals that Jesus Christ receives His eternal kingdom from the Father, the Antichrist is utterly crushed and handed over to God's court for his eternal doom (Dan. 7:26), and Christ will establish His kingdom (v. 27). Daniel wanted his people, and us, to know that God alone is sovereign over foreign affairs (Dan. 4:31–37).

The times of the Gentiles will end when Christ comes to rule, and we will rule with Him because the kingdom "will be given to the people of the saints of the Highest One" (Dan. 7:27). The exact identity of these people wasn't revealed to Daniel, but that's the church.

THE CHURCH

When Israel rejected and crucified its Messiah in fulfillment of Daniel's sixty-ninth week, God hit the clock for Israel and stopped the movement of the nation's prophetic program. But when God stopped the clock on Israel, He started the prophetic clock ticking for the Gentile world—and it's still running. The times of the Gentiles began with Israel's desolation in the sixty-ninth week when Jesus the Messiah was cut off, and they will continue until the tribulation. At that time, God will start the clock for Israel again and Daniel's seventieth week will unfold in the great tribulation.

What has God been doing since He stopped one prophetic clock and started another one? The primary thing He has been doing is building His church, a brand-new entity made up of Jews and Gentiles.

As I mentioned, the reason God stopped Israel's prophetic clock is that Israel rejected the Messiah who came to offer the nation the promises of the covenants God gave them in the Old Testament. Israel had promises of blessing, promises of land, and a descendant of David to sit on the throne.

But to receive these blessings, God's chosen people needed to receive Jesus as Messiah. They couldn't reject the King and expect to receive the kingdom. God's promises are sure, but in fulfilling them He does not disregard our participation and relational responsibilities in the process.

God can make you a promise in the Bible, but if you are not spiritually ready to receive it, He will put it on hold in your life until you are ready. God's promises are always there for His people, but we are not always prepared to claim them.

That does not mean God won't keep His promises. It just means that He keeps His promises not only when *He* is good and ready, but when *you* are good and ready. God's promises are prepared for you, but you must be prepared for His promises.

Crucifying the King

Jesus' rejection by the nation of Israel came from the onset of His ministry within many groups of Jewish people. He was rejected by the religious leaders of that day. Ultimately, this led to His crucifixion. Jesus foresaw this, of course, and with the cross ahead, He told "the chief priests and the elders of the people" (Matt. 21:23) a series of parables illustrating their rejection.

At one point, Jesus said, "Did you never read in the Scriptures, 'The stone which the builders rejected, this became the chief corner stone; this came about from the Lord, and it is marvelous in our eyes'? Therefore I say to you, the kingdom of God will be taken away from you and be given to a people, producing the fruit of it" (vv. 42–43).

Jesus prophesied His rejection and the postponement of Israel's kingdom. The Messiah was cut off at the end of the sixty-ninth week of Daniel's prophecy when Jesus died on the cross. Israel's prophetic clock came to a halt. But the program of God would go forward. After Jesus' death and resurrection, God was ready to introduce a new phase of His plan for the ages, a mystery called the church that had not been revealed to previous generations.

The Formation of the Church

To find the first mention of the church we have to turn back to Matthew 16:13–19. Jesus Christ went to Caesarea Philippi with His disciples and asked them what people were saying about Him.

After hearing the disciples' answers, Jesus asked, "But who do you say that I am?" Peter gave the right answer. "You are the Christ, the Son of the living God" (vv. 15–16). The truth Peter spoke led to a new prophecy from Jesus. "I also say to you that you are Peter, and upon this rock I will build My church; and the gates of Hades will not overpower it" (v. 18).

In this verse, Jesus announced for the first time the new plan of God that would unfold because of Israel's rejection. God was going to take a detour around Israel's unbelief, because He will never allow man's rebellion to thwart His kingdom program.

The church is a brand-new entity that had never existed before. The church is different from Israel because a person was an Israelite by virtue of physical birth and religious heritage. The Jews are a physical race of people. But the church is made up of people from all races who belong to Jesus Christ.

Jesus said, "I will build My church." This is something that Jesus would do Himself. It was yet future when He spoke these words, and it's a building process, which means it will take time.

This group will also belong to Christ personally. The church is the bride of Christ, whereas Israel was called the wife of God in the Old Testament. And this new work will bear the name *church*, meaning "called-out ones."

Once again, to set the church in its prophetic context, it is a gathered body of people who belong uniquely to Christ during the interval between the sixty-ninth and seventieth weeks of Daniel's prophecy, the period between the death and resurrection of Christ and the beginning of the tribulation.

Now let's look at Matthew 16:19. Jesus said, "I will give you the keys of the kingdom of heaven; and whatever you bind on earth shall have been bound in heaven, and whatever you loose on earth shall have been loosed in heaven."

Keys give access, and the church has the keys to the kingdom—which means access to God's program—because Israel refused the kingdom. The church is now the entity in history that has access to God, that can unlock heaven's doors. Those who refuse to accept Christ have no access to heaven. Only the church has the keys to God's kingdom.

The Church and Israel

This raises a question of the relationship between the church and Israel during this period called the church age when the prophetic clock has been stopped for Israel. Paul dealt with this important question in Romans 11, using the illustration of an olive tree:

> If [Israel's] rejection is the reconciliation of the world, what will their acceptance be but life from the dead? If the first piece of dough is holy, the lump is also; and if the root is holy, the branches are too.
>
> But if some of the branches were broken off, and you, being a wild olive, were grafted in among them and became partaker with them of the rich root of the olive tree, do not be arrogant toward the branches; but if you are arrogant, remember that it is not you who supports the root, but the root supports you. (vv. 15–18)

The olive tree is God's program or blessings. Israel was the natural branch because it was the first to enjoy God's blessings through Abraham. But the branch for unbelieving Israel was cut off, and the Gentiles were grafted in as a new branch. This new branch is the church, made up of Jews and Gentiles who have come to Christ and are brought together in a new body (Eph. 2:11–14).

Even though most believers today are not Jewish, we are enjoying the blessings of the Abrahamic covenant because God told Abraham, "In you all the families of the earth will be blessed" (Gen. 12:3). God promised to bless the whole world through Abraham. But now instead of bringing the blessing through Israel, He is doing it through the church.

The church is certainly unique and special in God's program, but Paul made sure we won't become arrogant about our position. As we read above, he cautioned Gentile believers against arrogance because their position in God's favor is only possible through His grace. Paul continued: "You will say then, 'Branches were broken off so that I might be grafted in.' Quite right, they were broken off for their unbelief, but you stand by your faith. Do not be conceited, but fear" (Rom. 11:19–20). Christians ought to be the humblest people on earth.

Israel's Temporary Rejection

Let's continue in Romans 11, where Paul showed that Israel's unbelief is not permanent. "For I do not want you, brethren, to be uninformed of this mystery—so that you will not be wise in your own estimation—that a partial hardening has happened to Israel until the fullness of the Gentiles has come in; and so all Israel will be saved" (vv. 25–26a).

In the Bible, a mystery is something that wasn't understood in the past, but is now revealed. The mystery Paul wanted the church to understand is that Israel's unbelief is temporary. He has not completely rejected His chosen people. Once the full number of Gentiles "has come in," or is born, God will bring Israel to Himself.

Israel was supposed to be the light of the world to bring the Gentiles to faith in God. But when Israel failed its mission, God set the nation aside and is now using the church to reach the world until all the Gentiles God has ordained to be born are born. And even though the rapture of the church will usher in a time of terrible suffering and persecution for Israel, God is going to turn the hearts of His chosen people to Christ at that time through those events. Then "all Israel will be saved."

That's why you can't, nor shouldn't, ignore the Middle East. Israel is going to stay on the front page of history and ought to capture the church's attention whenever events transpire there. Scripture gives us a wonderful template on how to pray for Israel where it is recorded in Psalm 122:6–9:

Pray for the peace of Jerusalem:
"May they prosper who love you.
"May peace be within your walls,
And prosperity within your palaces."
For the sake of my brothers and my friends,
I will now say, "May peace be within you."
For the sake of the house of the LORD our God,
I will seek your good.

David's song and prayer should be our own. Israel and the church are related even though they are distinct entities in God's kingdom agenda. They are both part of God's olive tree. Israel's unbelief and rejection of Christ is a temporary situation. God is not finished with Israel. Not at all.

PART TWO

The Coming of Prophesied Events

7

PROPHECY AND THE RAPTURE

The rapture is the next event in God's prophetic program, and it's time for us to talk about it as we fast-forward to the end of the church age. The term *rapture* comes from the Latin word for the Greek term translated "caught up" in 1 Thessalonians 4:17. We'll deal with this central passage as we unfold the doctrine of Christ's return in the air to take His bride, the church, home for the wedding.

THE IMPORTANCE OF THE RAPTURE

In the upper room the night before He was crucified, Jesus announced to His disciples that He was going to leave them. This threw them into consternation and fear, so Jesus gave them the reassuring promise of John 14:1–3, which concludes, "If I go and prepare a place for you, I will come again and receive you to Myself, that where I am, there you may be also."

This is the first clear reference to the return of Jesus for His own, the event described in 1 Thessalonians 4:13–18 that we call the rapture.

The fact of Jesus' prophetic promise, and the conditions under which He made it, make the rapture a very important teaching for the church.

The imagery Jesus used in the Gospels for His return at the rapture was that of a cultural wedding (see Matt. 25:1–13). The bridegroom would go away and prepare a place for his bride. Then when it was time for the wedding, he would come back for her and take her to be with him in the place he had prepared.

A Reason to Be Secure

One reason the rapture is so important is that the expectation of Christ's return means we don't have to be troubled (John 14:1).

We have a secure future in Christ even though we have to face troubling times, troubling situations, and troubling people. We can be calm in the face of trouble because Jesus Christ is coming back for His bride, and we'll be with Him forever.

The Answer to Jesus' Prayer

The rapture is also an important part of biblical prophecy because it is the answer to Jesus' prayer in John 17:24: "Father, I desire that they also, whom You have given Me, be with Me where I am, so that they may see My glory."

Jesus asked His Father to make arrangements so that those whom the Father had given to the Son—His bride, the church—could live with Christ. Jesus is going to claim His bride at the rapture. We will be the first to be with Him because the rapture will occur before the end-time events we have been studying.

In other words, when God ends time and ushers in eternity, all believers of all ages will go to live with God in heaven. But this is not what Jesus was talking about in John 17:24. He was requesting that the special ones God gave Him, which is the church, the bride of Christ, be allowed to go with Him.

Hope in the Face of Death

A third reason the rapture is important takes us to 1 Thessalonians 4:13–18, the key passage on this concept. I won't quote the entire passage here since we will deal with these verses in more detail later. For now let's notice the purpose for which God gave the revelation of the rapture. Paul wrote, "Therefore comfort one another with these words" (v. 18; see also 1 Thess. 5:11).

The truth of the rapture is designed to bring hope at what would otherwise be the most hopeless moment in life, when someone you love is taken into eternity.

For those loved ones who have "fallen asleep in Jesus" (1 Thess. 4:14)—who died as Christians—there is the certain hope that they will be resurrected, and we will see them again when Christ comes for His church.

A Glorious Future

First Thessalonians 4 was written in response to a concern these Christians had in relation to those who had died. One reason the Thessalonians were unclear about this question is that Paul was only able to spend a short time in Thessalonica (Acts 17:1–9). Paul's preaching caused quite a stir, and he had to leave town after a few weeks because the Jews were upset that he was preaching Jesus Christ.

The result was that the church in Thessalonica didn't have detailed instruction in Christian doctrine. They knew Christ was coming back, and they were looking for Him to come at any time. But when the Lord didn't come back right away and some of their fellow believers died, these people wondered what would happen to these dead saints when Christ did return. They were afraid they wouldn't see these people again, and they were disturbed.

That's why Paul started this section by saying, "But we do not want you to be uninformed, brethren, about those who are asleep, so that you will not grieve as do the rest who have no hope" (1 Thess. 4:13).

Paul wanted the Thessalonians to understand what God had in store for them.

Please notice that God does not want His people to be ignorant about the rapture because it is so important for us to know about our future. This knowledge not only gives us hope for the future, but it transforms our values on earth. When you have the right vision of tomorrow, it prepares you to live today.

Paul was not saying it's wrong for us to grieve when we lose a loved one. He didn't expect the Thessalonians to be unmoved by the losses they had suffered. But the difference for us as Christians is that ours is a hopeful sorrow instead of a hopeless sorrow. To die without Christ brings a sorrow that is not mixed with hope, since those who die apart from Christ are lost forever. But we will be reunited with believers who have died.

CHRIST'S RETURN FOR HIS CHURCH

Now that we have seen something of the importance this doctrine holds for us, let's dig a little deeper into 1 Thessalonians 4 and find out what's involved in the rapture of the church.

No Reason for Confusion

We don't want to get the rapture confused with what is usually called the second coming of Christ, which will occur at the end of the tribulation as He comes to earth to set up His kingdom.

There are a number of differences between these two appearances. At the rapture, Christ comes in the air, and believers rise to meet Him and go back to heaven. There is also a resurrection of the dead.

At His second coming, Christ rides out of heaven on a white horse with an army following Him, and He comes to the earth to judge, make war, and overthrow all earthly powers. He then rules for a thousand years from His throne in Jerusalem, and no resurrection occurs at the moment of His coming. The rapture and second coming are different events.

No Reason to Deny the Rapture

Paul continued in 1 Thessalonians 4, "For if we believe that Jesus died and rose again, even so God will bring with Him those who have fallen asleep in Jesus" (v. 14).

This is a powerful verse because it says the return of Christ is as certain as His death and resurrection. Notice how the verse ties our confidence in His return to our belief in His death and resurrection. This means if you believe in Easter, then you have no rationale for denying the rapture. If Jesus can get up from the dead, He can come back. If Easter is true and there is a resurrection, there is also a rapture. According to Paul, these two doctrines stand or fall together.

No Reason to Fear Death

If you asked people whether they feared death, most would probably say they do. It's a natural human fear. Paul calls death an enemy (1 Cor. 15:26). But for Christians, death is a defeated enemy, so for us to be gripped by the fear of death is irrational.

Follow me here. Since the dead are coming back with Jesus, that means they aren't in the place where they died, because Jesus is in heaven. The only way dead believers could come back with Jesus is if they are with Him in heaven.

That's exactly what the Bible teaches, because "to be absent from the body" is "to be at home with the Lord" (2 Cor. 5:8). That's why the Bible calls death "sleep" for believers. Death is not the cessation of existence. The moment a Christian dies, that person's spirit leaves the body and is immediately with the Lord. The body, not the soul, sleeps in death. In fact, at the rapture the souls of departed believers will come back with Christ to be joined to their eternal resurrection bodies.

Paul could talk about the dead being with Christ because the essence of your personhood is your soul, not your body. Your present body is just the house in which your soul is temporarily located.

Let me review many people's worst fear about death and why you will never experience that fear. People are afraid that in death they will be stuck in a box six feet under the ground with worms as company and total nothingness all around them.

Of course, nothing is further from the truth—both for believers *and* unbelievers. Unbelievers go somewhere immediately at death, but it is the place of torment and suffering (see Luke 16:19–31). We'll deal with this in more detail a little later.

But if you know Christ, before the doctor has a chance to pronounce you dead, you will be in the Lord's presence. You will not experience death for even one portion of a second.

No Reason to Doubt the Word

Paul wanted the Thessalonians to know that what he was telling them was authoritative revelation from God: "For this we say to you by the word of the Lord" (1 Thess. 4:15).

The reason Paul said this is that the rapture was not prophesied in the Old Testament. It is truth for the church age, which the Old Testament prophets did not foresee clearly or write about in detail. But the word of the Lord was just as authoritative through Paul as it was through the prophets, and the Thessalonians could count on it.

THE UNION AT THE RAPTURE

The truth Paul was about to reveal was the order of events in the rapture, and the fact that, when it was all over, believers both dead and alive would be reunited with each other and with the Lord.

Remember, the problem here was the Thessalonians' distress over friends and family members who had died. So the good news Paul had to bring was that there is going to be a reunion for Christians someday. He continued:

> We who are alive and remain until the coming of the Lord, will not precede those who have fallen asleep. For the Lord Himself will descend from heaven with a shout, with the voice of the archangel and with the trumpet of God, and the dead in Christ will rise first. (1 Thess. 4:15b–16)

Not only do believers who have died not miss out on the rapture, they get a head start on everybody else! Three distinct steps or events are mentioned here that signal the arrival of the rapture.

The shout was a military command from an army officer, giving instructions on what should be done. What will the Lord's shout at the rapture do? The best way to answer this is by looking at an actual biblical event in which Jesus shouted for a dead person to come alive. The incident is the resurrection of Lazarus of Bethany in John 11.

Jesus' dear friend Lazarus had died, but Jesus came to Bethany four days later to do something about it. After they had removed the gravestone, Jesus prayed and then "cried out with a loud voice, 'Lazarus, come forth.' The man who had died came forth, bound hand and foot with wrappings, and his face was wrapped around with a cloth. Jesus said to them, 'Unbind him, and let him go'" (John 11:43–44).

Why did it take a loud command to resurrect Lazarus? Because death is the domain of Satan. He's the king of the grave. Death only exists because of satanically inspired sin.

Jesus overruled Satan by giving a command in enemy territory, and Lazarus came walking out of the grave. The same thing will happen at the rapture. When Christ comes in the air and issues His shout, the body of every believer who has fallen asleep in Jesus will exit the grave.

The second event Paul revealed in 1 Thessalonians 4:16 is the "voice of the archangel." Michael is the only archangel specifically mentioned in the Bible. What does he have to do with this? Well, "archangel" means the chief angel, the one in charge. Satan was the original chief angel in heaven when he was named Lucifer. But when he rebelled against God and was judged, Michael was apparently promoted and given the post.

Throughout the Bible we read of conflict between Michael and Satan at key points in biblical history (see Dan. 10:13, 21; Jude 9; Rev. 12:7–9). Michael as the head of the righteous angels seeks to carry out the will of God, and Satan as the head of the unrighteous angels seeks to stop God's will.

Michael is going to be on the scene with Christ at the rapture. When Jesus issues the command for the resurrection, Michael is going to tell his righteous angels, "You heard what the Lord said. Go get those dead believers and escort them through Satan's territory to heaven."

How do I know the angels are coming as heavenly escorts at the rapture? Because of the story of the rich man and Lazarus, which I alluded to earlier (Luke 16:19–31).

When the righteous beggar Lazarus died, Jesus said he "was carried away by the angels to Abraham's bosom" (v. 22), which is a term for heaven that was used before the death and resurrection of Christ.

Every believer has a guardian angel, so at the rapture we will each have an angelic escort to meet Jesus in the air. That's what happens at a wedding. The bride never comes to meet her bridegroom alone. She is escorted by attendants.

I can hear someone saying at this point, "Tony, I'm confused. Earlier you said the moment we die we go to be with Jesus, so we're already in heaven when the rapture comes. But now you're saying we will come out of the grave if we're not alive when Jesus comes for us. Which is true?"

The answer is both, because while your spirit is in heaven, at the rapture it will be joined to a new, resurrected, immortal, glorified body like the body Jesus had after His resurrection. That's why Paul could say we are coming back with Jesus (1 Thess. 4:14), and yet those in the grave will be resurrected.

The rapture is the day when we will be rid of our aging, sick, sore, sin-contaminated bodies forever! At that time, it won't matter if your old body was cremated or lost at sea or whatever, because the God who made you the first time out of dust knows exactly where all the parts are and how to put you back together again. For God, putting you back together is no harder than putting you together the first time.

Thus, at the rapture the Lord will descend from heaven with a shouted command of resurrection, and the angels will be there to escort us to heaven and make sure there is no hindrance from the demonic realm.

Then we have the third event in the rapture, "the trumpet of God" (1 Thess. 4:16). In the Bible a trumpet was used for two reasons, to call the people either to worship or to war. This trumpet call is to both.

It's a call to worship because once we get to heaven our occupation for eternity will be worshiping God. But the trumpet of God is also a call to war because we will come back with Him at the Battle of Armageddon, when the armies of heaven will ride out with Jesus in the lead (Rev. 19:11–16).

I don't know exactly how the shout, the voice of the archangel, and the trumpet will occur, whether they happen in order or all at once. But they summon us to the reunion: "The dead in Christ will rise first. Then we who are alive and remain will be caught up together with them in the clouds to meet the Lord in the air, and so we shall always be with the Lord" (1 Thess. 4:16b–17).

THE RESURRECTION OF THE BODY

One of the key elements of prophecy is the Bible's teaching that believers in Jesus Christ will enter eternity with new bodies fitted for eternal life in heaven. The issue that led Paul to mention resurrection in 1 Thessalonians 4 was a lack of information about the future. But in 1 Corinthians 15, his fullest teaching on the subject, Paul was addressing a problem that came about because of the influence of Greek culture on the first century world.

Corinth was greatly influenced by Greek thought. Basically the Greeks taught dualism, or a strict separation of spirit and matter. To the Greeks, spirit was good, but matter, including the human body, was evil. The Greeks could think great thoughts and live completely debauched lives because they believed the material side of life was meaningless.

Therefore, the idea of a bodily resurrection was foolishness to the Greeks. That's why most of Paul's hearers sneered when he mentioned the resurrection during his famous sermon in Athens (Acts 17:31–32). The Greeks rejected the idea of a resurrection, and the church began to buy into that philosophy of the age rather than believe what God had said.

An Illustration of the Resurrection

That may be why Paul devoted 1 Corinthians 15, one of the longest chapters in the New Testament, to the truth of the resurrection. I want to pick up his argument beginning in verse 35:

> But someone will say, "How are the dead raised? And with what kind of body do they come?" You fool! That which you sow does not come to life unless it dies; and that which you sow, you do not sow the body which is to be, but a bare grain, perhaps of wheat or of something else. But God gives it a body just as He wished, and to each of the seeds a body of its own. (vv. 35–38)

Paul anticipated the objection of someone who was arguing against the idea of a physical resurrection. He called this hypothetical person a fool for not recognizing a simple fact of nature that can be observed every day.

Basically, Paul was saying, "Somebody bring this guy some wheat seeds and remind him how those seeds grow and produce grain. They have to be planted in the ground and die in order for the new life of the grain to grow."

Paul's analogy made the point that the only way a new resurrected body could grow was for the old body to be buried in the ground in death. Unless the seed is buried, the grain will never grow. Death is required for new life to appear.

What is true of seeds is also true of our physical bodies that God has created. And what is true in the physical realm is also true in the spiritual. That is, death brings forth life. Christ had to die so you and I could live.

Paul also used the example of a grain seed (1 Cor. 15:37) to demonstrate the fact that our resurrection bodies will be very different from our earthly bodies. We have just talked about this, so let me point out the self-evident truth of what the apostle was saying.

Choose almost any fruit or vegetable or grain, and you can see that the body that grows out of the ground is very different from the "body" that was planted. Compare a pumpkin seed with a pumpkin, for example, or an orange seed with an orange.

Paul was not talking about the appearance of our resurrection bodies in terms of whether we will be recognizable. We dealt with that above. Paul's point was that the body that is planted in death is not the same body that is resurrected—and for that, most of us will be eternally grateful!

Natural and Spiritual Bodies

The fundamental difference between the bodies we have now and the bodies we will receive at the rapture is summarized for us in

1 Corinthians 15:44: "It is sown a natural body, it is raised a spiritual body. If there is a natural body, there is also a spiritual body."

The difference is natural versus spiritual. Now when Paul said it would be a spiritual body, he didn't mean merely an ethereal concept. Jesus' resurrection body had flesh and bones, and He ate a piece of fish in the disciples' presence (Luke 24:39, 42–43). But He was able to do things, such as pass through closed doors, that can't be done in a natural, or earthly, body.

You have the body your parents gave you through the process of natural birth. They did the best they could, but it still has problems. Besides the fact that our spiritual bodies will not be subject to the limitations of time, space, disease, etc., they will also enable us to see and enter into the realities of the spiritual world around us. For instance, the Bible teaches that we are surrounded by spiritual beings and spiritual activity. We've already said that each believer has at least one angel whose job it is to minister to that person. There are angels all over the place, but we cannot detect this activity because we are in our natural bodies.

However, when we receive our spiritual, resurrected bodies we will get to witness angelic systems at work. And we will experience the presence of God in a way that we cannot do today in our limited human bodies, since God is a spirit. That's why when you get to heaven you will learn more about God than you could possibly learn down here.

Faster than a Blink

But Paul wasn't finished teaching on the resurrection. "Behold, I tell you a mystery; we will not all sleep, but we will all be changed, in a moment, in the twinkling of an eye, at the last trumpet; for the trumpet will sound, and the dead will be raised imperishable, and we will be changed" (1 Cor. 15:51–52).

Notice that the order here is the same as in 1 Thessalonians 4: The dead are raised first, and then the living will receive their resurrection bodies. How fast will all this happen? The Greek word for *moment* is the word from which we get the English word "atom." For years the atom was thought to be the smallest, most irreducible part of matter. They've now split the atom, but the point is still made that the time it will take for Christ to rapture His church is infinitesimally small.

The twinkling of an eye is the time it takes for your eye to catch light, which is a lot faster than a blink. We will be changed and given our new bodies instantly.

THREE VIEWS ON THE TIME OF THE RAPTURE

There are three basic views on the timing of the rapture. Some believe it will occur before the tribulation and mark the beginning of this prophesied seven-year period.

Others believe the rapture will come at the midpoint of the tribulation, just as the Antichrist breaks his peace treaty with Israel, eradicates religion and demands to be worshiped as God, and all hell breaks loose on earth.

The third position is that the church will have to go through the tribulation, but will be supernaturally protected during that time and raptured at the end of the tribulation.

These three positions are logically known as pre-, mid-, and post-tribulationalism. I am a pre-tribulationalist because I believe the Bible teaches that Christ is coming for His church prior to the beginning of the tribulation, but I would encourage you to study and explore all three views and come to your own conclusion. For now, let me share mine.

Jesus' Promise to the Church

I am a pre-tribulationalist because I believe this is the promise Jesus made to the faithful church of Philadelphia, which is representative of the true church in all ages. The Lord said in Revelation 3:10, "Because you have kept the word of My perseverance, I also will keep you from the hour of testing, that hour which is about to come upon the whole world, to test those who dwell on the earth."

The "hour of testing" is the tribulation. Jesus used this terminology to describe the tribulation because He was saying the church is going to be kept from the very time frame in which the tribulation will occur.

To be kept "from," or "out of," a situation is different than being kept "through" it. The preposition translated "from" in Revelation 3:10 suggests the church will not be around when the tribulation breaks loose.

The Church in Heaven

It's also worth noting that immediately after this promise, Revelation 4 begins describing the time of God's final judgment on earth. But the church is nowhere to be found amid all the horrors that a righteous God is going to unleash on a sinful earth and the people who dwell on it.

The best explanation for the church's absence from Revelation 4 until the kingdom and the marriage supper of the Lamb in Revelation 20–21 is that the church will be raptured before the tribulation begins.

The Bible also promises that as God's people, we will be delivered "from the wrath to come" (1 Thess. 1:10). God's wrath here is not only hell, but the tribulation period. Later in 1 Thessalonians, Paul said, "The day of the Lord [the day of God's judgment in the tribulation] will come just like a thief in the night" (5:2). But then Paul said to the church, "But you, brethren, are not in darkness, that the day should overtake you like a thief" (v. 4). And finally we have this promise: "For God has not destined us for wrath, but for obtaining salvation through our Lord Jesus Christ" (v. 9).

The Revelation of the Antichrist

Let me offer another rationale for the pre-tribulational position. When Paul wrote 2 Thessalonians, the believers there were all shook up again, this time because false teachers there were saying the day of the Lord had already started (2 Thess. 2:1–2). But Paul said:

> Let no one in any way deceive you, for it will not come unless the apostasy comes first, and the man of lawlessness is revealed, the son of destruction, who opposes and exalts himself above every so-called god or object of worship, so that he takes his seat in the temple of God, displaying himself as being God. . . . And you know what restrains him now, so that in his time he will be revealed. For the mystery of lawlessness is already at work; only he who now restrains will do so until he is taken out of the way. Then that lawless one will be revealed. (vv. 3–4, 6–8a)

The Thessalonians were rattled because if the tribulation had begun, that meant they had been left behind in the rapture. But Paul set their end times theology straight, and in the process made clear the order of events.

The tribulation will not begin until the Antichrist, who is described so vividly in these verses, is revealed. And he won't be revealed until the restrainer, the Holy Spirit, is taken off the earth.

Follow the reasoning here. The Holy Spirit dwells in the church. He came at Pentecost to take up His residence in the body of believers who make up the church. In fact, it is Holy Spirit baptism that marks a person as a member of Christ's body the church (1 Cor. 12:13).

So if the tribulation doesn't begin until the Antichrist is revealed, and if he won't be revealed until after the Holy Spirit leaves, guess who leaves when the Spirit leaves? The church!

Based on these passages, I don't expect the church to go through the tribulation. Before a nation attacks a foreign country, one of the things the attacking nation often does is remove its citizens from that foreign country.

We've seen this happen many times just in the last few decades. The US removed her citizens from places where there would be planned military involvement. The same principle operates in heaven. Jesus Christ is going to bring the citizens of heaven home before God executes His fierce wrath on the earth.

A CHALLENGE TO FAITHFULNESS

The good news of the rapture should be comforting to believers (1 Thess. 4:18; see 5:11). But let me also leave you with a word of challenge. The shout and the trumpet call could come at any time. We could be caught away to meet the Lord in the air today. What should that knowledge do for us? Paul answered that in the last verse of 1 Corinthians 15. "Therefore, my beloved brethren, be steadfast, immovable, always abounding in the work of the Lord, knowing that your toil is not in vain in the Lord" (v. 58).

The knowledge of Christ's soon return should motivate us to serve Him fully and faithfully, especially in light of the judgment seat of Christ. It should lead to holiness of life on our part because the Bible also says, "Everyone who has this hope fixed on [Christ] purifies himself, just as He is pure" (1 John 3:3).

If you knew Jesus was coming back at this time next year, would you be doing some things differently today? The judgment seat of Christ pertains only to Christians, and is not related at all to the final judgment in which all nonbelievers are sent to their eternal destiny.

If you know Jesus Christ as your Savior, your judgment in terms of heaven and hell has already been decided. Christ paid for your sins and experienced your hell on the cross, and He purchased heaven for you. The rapture will take all who are in Christ to be with Him—and anyone who is left behind at the rapture has another problem altogether.

The purpose of Christ's judgment seat is to judge or evaluate us for the way we lived our Christian lives, for the quality of our service.

The question here is not whether you are a Christian, but what kind of Christian you are.

From the standpoint of God's prophetic plan, the judgment seat of Christ is the first order of business for the church after the rapture. Since we know we are going to be evaluated, how can we prepare? Understanding prophecy and what is to come ought to impact our choices each moment of each day. As kingdom followers of Jesus Christ, saved by His blood, we will stand before Him one day at His judgment seat. Recognizing this as truth should influence your decisions while living here on earth. It should encourage you to live with a kingdom worldview and an eternal perspective, sharing the hope and message of the gospel with all you can.

8

PROPHECY AND THE ANTICHRIST

Now that we've spent some time concentrating on the church's place in the prophetic plan of God, including the future awaiting us in the rapture and Christ's judgment seat, we need to bring our attention back to earth, so to speak.

Next, I want to examine the events that will unfold once the restraining influence of the church and the Holy Spirit is removed from the earth. It's not a pretty picture, because what we're talking about here is the tribulation, the seven-year period of God's judgment that begins after the rapture and constitutes the seventieth week of Daniel's prophecy. More specifically, this period will feature the unveiling of the person first mentioned in the book of Daniel—the incarnation of Satan himself, the Antichrist.

We'll do some review of Daniel along the way, but you may want to go back and refresh yourself on his prophecy of the seventy weeks. This is Israel's prophetic history, a 490-year span of time that began with the decree given to Nehemiah to rebuild Jerusalem and that ground to a halt when Messiah, Jesus Christ, was "cut off" (Dan. 9:26) at His crucifixion.

We pointed out that the seventieth week of Daniel's prophecy—the final seven years of God's prophetic plan for His people—has never been fulfilled. That's because God stopped the clock and called "timeout" on Israel after Calvary. The tribulation starts Israel's clock ticking again.

A ticking clock is a good analogy for the seven-year period called the tribulation, because Satan's time bomb is just waiting to explode in unrestrained evil on the world, and on Israel in particular. This will happen at the midpoint of the seven years when his "star," the Antichrist, reveals himself for who he is, and all hell breaks loose on the earth.

Now if you think sin has the upper hand in the world today, you haven't seen anything yet. There's a lot Satan can't do because the church is still here resisting sin, and because saints are on their knees praying. Satan is restrained in carrying out his evil plans by the person of the Holy Spirit who indwells the church.

But imagine what this world would be like if the devil were free to work his evil with no restraints. That's the definition of the tribulation, and especially the last three-and-a-half years, which the Bible calls the "great tribulation." God will take the shackles off Satan and unleash His wrath on the earth.

Satan's "superstar" who will rule in the tribulation is known by several names. Daniel called him "another horn, a little one," "a king [who is] insolent," and "the prince who is to come" (Dan. 7:8; 8:23; 9:26). He is also called "the man of lawlessness" and "the son of destruction" (2 Thess. 2:3), and the Beast (Rev. 13:1). But the name that sums up this person's character is "the Antichrist" (1 John 2:18). He will be against Christ and will seek to undermine and imitate the Son of God. Let's look at the Antichrist's rise to power, the evil nature of his rule, and the condemnation in store for him.

THE CONTEXT FOR THE ANTICHRIST

History teaches us that powerful rulers don't just arise out of nowhere. They come to the fore within a certain context, a set of conditions that prepares the way for their coming. Any cursory glance at current events in the Middle East both now or in the past will reveal a context open and ripe for the rise of an "antichrist." This is a leader who shows up to seemingly save the day. The world in which we live has turned into such chaos at times that it is only natural to look for somebody who will rise to the scene to bring order to a chaotic world.

The Biblical Context

We've already discussed Daniel 7 in some detail, but we need to review some verses to set the context for the rise of Antichrist. Daniel wrote:

> After this I kept looking in the night visions, and behold, a fourth beast, dreadful and terrifying and extremely strong; and it had large iron teeth. It devoured and crushed and trampled down the remainder with its feet; and it was different from all the beasts that were before it, and it had ten horns. While I was contemplating the horns, behold, another horn, a little one, came up among them, and three of the first horns were pulled out by the roots before it; and behold, this horn possessed eyes like the eyes of a man and a mouth uttering great boasts. (vv. 7–8)

God gave Daniel a vision of four powerful beasts that would arise and rule the world. This prophecy was fulfilled in the Gentile world powers of Babylon, Medo-Persia, Greece, and Rome. King Nebuchadnezzar had had a similar dream earlier, seeing a statue of a man with legs of iron and feet of iron and clay (Dan. 2:33). This statue also outlined the four major Gentile powers that would dominate the Middle East. The ten toes of Nebuchadnezzar's statue, which symbolized the breakup of the Roman Empire, are called the "ten horns" in Daniel 7. It is out of these horns, or rulers, that the little horn, the Antichrist, will arise.

The Revival of Rome's Empire

The old Roman Empire was divided and eventually fell apart in fulfillment of biblical prophecy. The ultimate result of this breakup was the formation of the various nations in Europe, as I noted in the chapter on Daniel's prophecy. But the Bible also prophesies a future revival of the Roman Empire.

For many years skeptics dismissed this prophecy because for hundreds of years Europe has been divided into sovereign kingdoms and nations that fought each other to maintain their independence or conquer and rule their neighbors.

But in 1989, the Berlin Wall fell, and Germany was reunified. And then the European economic union emerged, and we now have something called the euro, a common currency to be used over most of Europe. The nations in the union have surrendered their currencies to unite under one standard. Suddenly, the picture of a reunified Europe has taken shape. Of course this has been challenged over the years as well, and some nations have left. But the concept of a unified Europe remains stronger than ever before. Any student of medieval history must be astonished by the unity amongst those who used to kill, siege, and destroy each other as part of their own survival.

The Bible says this process of unification will ultimately come down to a ten-nation alliance, out of which the little horn, or Antichrist, will emerge. Horns are a symbol of power in the Bible, so his power will be small at first. I take it the world won't notice the Antichrist when he first begins making his move.

Daniel said this being will have "eyes like the eyes of a man"—a reference to human intelligence and knowledge. Antichrist will arise and uproot or overthrow three of the ten kingdoms of the revived Roman Empire.

We don't know how or when this will occur, because we don't know when Christ is coming back. But the context is there in Europe, the stage is set, for the Antichrist to seize control.

The Technology for Control

People also used to wonder how the Antichrist would ever be able to imprint the number 666 on people so that he could wield absolute economic control. But in the day and age we live in now, that is not difficult to comprehend at all. We are in the era of technological advancement and artificial intelligence. The lockdowns that happened as a result of the COVID-19 epidemic revealed to us the ability some nations have to control people's movements based on technology. You hear people debating the morality of a "social credit score" which either enables or prevents the user from purchasing needed items such as food and water. Nothing stands in the way of the imprinting of 666 onto individuals any longer, at least not from a technological standpoint.

Chaos and Desire for Peace

The deterioration of civilization we are seeing today will increase greatly after the church has been raptured. The chaos will become such that the human race will cry out for a leader who can impose order and bring peace to the world.

Our world today is longing for peace. Imagine how the world would embrace a leader who could step up and settle the age-old conflict in the Middle East with one stroke of brilliant diplomacy. Imagine how people would welcome someone who could give them economic stability in return for a little more control over their lives. History proves that people will surrender their rights for stability and a sense of peace in times of chaos. Our most recent history of the global lockdowns showed this on a large scale.

The Antichrist will be able to deliver peace and stability, and the unbelieving world will welcome him as he spends the first three-and-a-half years of the tribulation solidifying his power and gaining control.

This leader will be able to bring all peoples together and appear to be able to end racial conflict, ethnic cleansing, class destruction, and religious tensions. The conditions are ripe for the emergence of such a leader.

THE CHARACTER OF THE ANTICHRIST

The world kingdoms that Daniel saw were characterized as beasts. It was out of the fourth beast that the Antichrist arose, and he is more beastly than all the others.

Satan's "Incarnate One"
> Then I saw a beast coming up out of the sea, having ten horns and seven heads, and on his horns were ten diadems, and on his heads were blasphemous names. And the beast which I saw was like a leopard, and his feet were like those of a bear, and his mouth like the mouth of a lion. (Rev. 13:1b–2b)

The beast John saw is the Antichrist—fast like a leopard, strong like a bear, and boastful like a lion roaring to assert its power. He comes out of the sea, which in this kind of setting refers to the Gentiles as opposed to the Jews, who come from the land of Israel.

So the Beast will be a Gentile. The "diadems" or crowns the Beast is wearing are ten nations over which he will rule.

It's clear where the Antichrist gets his power. "The dragon gave him his power and his throne and great authority" (v. 2b). The Dragon is none other than Satan, so identified by John in Revelation 12:9. The Antichrist's program is described in the following verses of chapter 13. "I saw one of his heads as if it had been slain, and his fatal wound was healed. And the whole earth was amazed and followed after the beast; they worshiped the dragon because he gave his authority to the beast" (vv. 3–4a).

Does this pattern sound familiar? Satan is imitating God the Father and Jesus Christ, whose job it is to lead mankind to the worship of God. More than anything else, Satan wanted to be worshiped like God. That was his original sin (Isa. 14).

Satan failed in his rebellion, but in the Antichrist he will have his own false messiah, his incarnate one, who will reflect his character and cause the unbelieving world to worship Satan.

A Prideful Beast

The Antichrist will also inspire worship (Rev. 13:4b), and will spew out his pride:

> There was given to him a mouth speaking arrogant words and blasphemies, and authority to act for forty-two months was given to him. And he opened his mouth in blasphemies against God, to blaspheme His name and His tabernacle, that is, those who dwell in heaven. (vv. 5–6)

Why does the Antichrist blaspheme God? Because the great sin of the Beast's spiritual father, Satan, was pride. So the Beast is going to reflect his father's character. That's why God hates pride above all other sins (Prov. 6:16–17). It reminds Him of Satan and his rebellion in heaven.

The Beast is granted power for forty-two months, the three-and-a-half years that make up the last half of the tribulation. This period is the great tribulation, as we noted above, the time when evil incarnate breaks loose on the earth.

A Lawless Beast

Paul showed what will happen when the restraint of the Holy Spirit and the church has been removed:

Then that lawless one will be revealed whom the Lord will slay with the breath of His mouth and bring to an end by the appearance of His coming; that is, the one whose coming is in accord with the activity of Satan, with all power and signs and false wonders. (2 Thess. 2:8–9)

This lawless one is the Antichrist, the offspring of the devil. Notice that he can work miracles. Some people get all excited about miracles, but don't jump too quickly. The devil can produce miracles and signs, for the wrong purpose: "And with all the deception of wickedness for those who perish, because they did not receive the love of the truth so as to be saved" (v. 10).

The old laws and old rules won't mean anything when the Antichrist shows up. He will write his own constitution, pass his own laws. We are talking about a world leader.

A Violent Beast

We'll see later that the Antichrist will also rule by violence. Anyone who doesn't accept his mark will die of starvation. He will rule in the great tribulation with an iron fist. When faced with a choice of resisting and dying or giving in and eating, most people will choose to eat. So those on the earth will be caught in a very traumatic situation. The Antichrist will use violence for his purposes—and we shouldn't be surprised, knowing who his spiritual father is. The Antichrist will be the very image of Satan.

THE CONDUCT OF THE ANTICHRIST

Let's look at the conduct of the Antichrist. What will he do during his time on the earth? The Bible shows that the Antichrist is a true "Dr. Jekyll and Mr. Hyde," because when he first appears on the scene he comes as a man of peace, a true Nobel Peace Prize winner, bringing peace to the Middle East. Everybody will love him.

A Deceitful Peacemaker

Daniel wrote concerning the Antichrist's activity, "He will make a firm covenant with the many for one week" (Dan. 9:27). This "week" is Daniel's seventieth week, the final period of seven years, which is still future. The covenant is a seven-year peace treaty the Antichrist will make with Israel that will seem to settle the Middle East conflict. This charismatic, powerful, attractive leader will do what other world leaders couldn't do—get the Arabs and Israelis to the peace table and hammer out a treaty. And guess what else he will do? He will give the Jews back their temple and make it possible for them to start offering sacrifices again.

This is very important to understand. The Jews lost their temple and their ability to offer sacrifices when the Roman general Titus destroyed Jerusalem in AD 70. The only part of the temple left standing today is the Western Wall, often called the "wailing wall" because Jews pray at this wall and lament the destruction of their temple, praying that God will restore the temple so they can start up the sacrificial system again.

But there's one huge problem. A Muslim mosque sits on the Temple Mount, Mount Moriah where Abraham offered up Isaac. During the Gulf War, the orthodox Jews were praying that a Scud missile would hit that mosque because it has to go before the temple can be rebuilt. Orthodox Jews are praying for the Messiah to come and give them back their place of worship. Of course, since the Messiah has come, worship is no longer tied to a place but to a person (John 4:21–24). But the Antichrist will give the Jews what they ask for. They will be allowed to rebuild their temple and offer sacrifices once again.

When all of this comes to pass the world will be saying, "Peace and safety!" (1 Thess. 5:3) and singing the Antichrist's praises because finally, there is peace. He will be a hero. People will wonder where this man has been all their lives. He will appear out of nowhere and do astounding things.

Solidifying His Power

The Antichrist will also use the first half of the tribulation to solidify his power in preparation for his world takeover. He will be a masterful schemer, because he will control the powerful forces of politics and religion, fusing them into one entity to serve his will.

We mentioned above that the Antichrist's political and economic control will be so complete that anyone who does not accept his mark cannot carry on a normal life (Rev. 13:16–18). We've spent some time on this part of the Antichrist's reign of terror, so I want to examine his use of religion to further Satan's plan.

In Revelation 17, an angel showed John "the great harlot who sits on many waters" (v. 1). She is further described as "a woman sitting on a scarlet beast, full of blasphemous names, having seven heads and ten horns" (v. 3). The prostitute was beautifully adorned and committed adulteries with the kings of the earth.

The identity of the Beast on which the woman was riding is given for us later in the chapter. Clearly, this is the Antichrist (vv. 8–11). The woman represents false religion that will be left on earth after the rapture and will join with the Antichrist because he has enriched the coffers of the false religious leaders.

When the Bible speaks of false religion, worship that is unfaithful to God, it often does so using the imagery of adultery or sexual immorality. God often complained to Israel that she was an unfaithful wife to Him by worshiping other gods (cf. the book of Hosea). The Israelites prostituted themselves to idols.

The woman of Revelation 17 is world religion, carrying right on as if nothing had happened after the true church is raptured. Not only that, but the religion of the tribulation will be ecumenical, all the world's religions coming together as one under the generous sponsorship of the Antichrist.

Notice that John saw this woman riding the Beast. The Antichrist will be the supporter of religion gone bad. He will be the head of this outfit. So here is a world figure, inspired by Satan, the very incarnation of evil, holding the reins of total political and religious control. This is religion in bed with politics, playing the prostitute for wealth and influence.

Once the Antichrist has total political and religious control, he will be ready for his unveiling, the great tribulation, when Satan pulls off the mask and shows the world his true nature. It is as though God is saying, "You wanted a world without Me. Now you have it. Satan, the earth is yours."

At this point human civilization will come full circle back to the goals of those who built the Tower of Babel (Gen. 11). There mankind came together to build a one-world government without God. But what the builders of Babel failed to do, the Antichrist will pull off for a while.

Once the Antichrist has solidified his power, he won't need organized religion anymore. So later in Revelation 17 we learn, "And the ten horns [ten kings] which you saw, and the beast, these will hate the harlot and will make her desolate and naked, and will eat her flesh and will burn her up with fire" (v. 16).

You see, Satan doesn't mind religion as long as he can use it. But his ultimate purpose is to wipe out all vestiges of worship to God and usurp God's place on the throne. The great tribulation is the closest

Satan will come to his age-old desire, because for that brief period he will be the object of people's worship through the Antichrist.

Demanding Worship

In the middle of Daniel's seventieth week (Dan. 9:27), or the midpoint of the tribulation, the Antichrist will use his control to demand worldwide worship (Rev. 13:8).

This in itself is not unusual. The ancient Romans worshiped their emperor as a god. To be a loyal Roman citizen, you had to offer a pinch of incense to Caesar and declare, "Caesar is Lord." It's not unusual today to see people worshiping their political leaders. But the Antichrist will take this further than anyone.

The Antichrist's sudden attack on religion will commence with his desecration of the rebuilt temple in Jerusalem, the halting of the daily sacrifices, and the establishment of "the abomination of desolation" (Dan. 11:31; cf. 9:27). Jesus warned His listeners to run for the hills when they saw this abomination standing in the temple (Matt. 24:15–16).

Now the wraps are off and the Antichrist is revealed in all of his evil. In the holy place of the temple, where the sacrifices are offered, an image of the Antichrist will be set up and he will be proclaimed as God. He will demand not only political loyalty, but worship. And the penalty for anyone who refuses will be death. Satan will finally have his false Christ and the worship he has always wanted (Rev. 13:4).

THE COMPANION OF THE ANTICHRIST

So far we have met two unholy beings, Satan and the Antichrist. But there is a third member of this evil trinity, because Satan wants to imitate God in every way. God is Father, Son, and Holy Spirit, so Satan has his version of the Trinity, the unholy trinity of himself, the Antichrist, and the False Prophet.

The Antichrist's "Energizer"

In Revelation 13, we are also introduced to this third member of the evil trio, later called "the false prophet" (Rev. 16:13).

John wrote: "Then I saw another beast coming up out of the earth; and he had two horns like a lamb and he spoke as a dragon. He exercises all the authority of the first beast in his presence. And he makes the earth and those who dwell in it to worship the first beast" (Rev. 13:11–12).

The job of this Satan-inspired creature will be to mimic the Holy Spirit's relationship to Christ. The Holy Spirit's role is to bring praise and worship to Christ, so the False Prophet's assignment will be to bring praise and worship to the false Christ, the Antichrist.

John saw this beastly figure coming up out of the earth as opposed to the Antichrist, who arose out of the sea. The sea represents the Gentile nations in prophecy, but the earth refers to the land of Israel. So this probably means the False Prophet will be of Jewish origin, or at least come out of the Middle East.

A Miracle Worker

How will the False Prophet inspire people to worship the Antichrist openly? Please take careful note of his method.

> He performs great signs, so that he even makes fire come down out of heaven to the earth in the presence of men. And he deceives those who dwell on the earth because of the signs which it was given him to perform. (Rev. 13:13–14)

When a person who claims divine power is able to make fire fall from heaven at his command, who is going to step up and deny that? Not the people on earth during the great tribulation. Because they didn't believe the truth, they will be vulnerable to Satan's lie. The False Prophet's miracles are part of the deception.

Let me stop here for a minute and remind you of what I said earlier about miracles. Don't get too excited too fast about the miraculous. Not every miracle is from God. Satan has a few tricks of his own, and the False Prophet will know how to use them.

This guy will just be getting warmed up by making fire come down from heaven. He will perform a far greater miracle: "It was given to him to give breath to the image of the beast, so that the image of the beast would even speak and cause as many as do not worship the image of the beast to be killed" (Rev. 13:15).

This image is the abomination of desolation we talked about above, a statue of the Antichrist set up in the temple in Jerusalem to be worshiped as God. The False Prophet will bring this statue to life, and anyone who doesn't fall down before it will be put to death.

The False Prophet's next assignment is to oversee the application of the mark of the Beast (vv. 16–18). By this time, very few people will have the courage to resist the Antichrist, and those who refuse the mark will pay with their lives.

Everybody loves to speculate about the meaning of the number 666. People have tried to tie it to the names of various figures in history so we will know who the Antichrist is. But I have a much simpler explanation for the significance of 666. In the Bible, six is the number of man. Man was created on the sixth day. He was commanded to work six days, and to rest on the seventh day and worship God. Six is close to seven, the number of God and the number of perfection in the Bible.

The threefold repetition of the number six in Revelation 13:18 represents the three members of Satan's unholy trinity: himself, the Beast, and the False Prophet. The number six is man trying to be God, but never arriving. The number 666 is a threefold expression of the entities in the satanic trinity.

THE CONDEMNATION OF THE BEAST

The Antichrist's reign as Satan's world ruler will come to an abrupt end after three-and-a-half years, so let's talk about the judgment of the Beast. We'll deal with this in more detail later, so let's just review it briefly for now.

Defeat for the Antichrist will come swiftly and totally when Jesus Christ rides out of heaven with His armies:

> And I saw the beast and the kings of the earth and their armies assembled to make war against Him who sat on the horse and against His army.
>
> And the beast was seized, and with him the false prophet who performed the signs in his presence, by which he deceived those who had received the mark of the beast and those who worshiped his image; these two were thrown alive into the lake of fire which burns with brimstone. (Rev. 19:19–20)

When Jesus comes back, that will be it for the Antichrist. His beastly days will be over because number six will have run into number seven! Jesus Christ will destroy the Antichrist with the sword that comes out of His mouth (v. 21).

SOME LESSONS WE NEED TO LEARN

You may be saying, "Tony, if the church is going to be raptured before the great tribulation, then I really don't need to know about all of this."

That's not what the Bible says. Consider these warnings from the apostle John, written to the church:

> Children, it is the last hour; and just as you heard that antichrist is coming, even now many antichrists have appeared;

from this we know that it is the last hour. . . . Who is the liar but the one who denies that Jesus is the Christ? This is the antichrist, the one who denies the Father and the Son. . . . And every spirit that does not confess Jesus is not from God; this is the spirit of the antichrist, of which you have heard that it is coming, and now it is already in the world. . . . For many deceivers have gone out into the world, those who do not acknowledge Jesus Christ as coming in the flesh. This is the deceiver and the antichrist. (1 John 2:18, 22; 4:3; 2 John 7)

The spirit of deception and denial that will ultimately lead to the worship of Antichrist is already among us. There are deceivers out there now, "little antichrists" trying to lead God's people astray.

So we had better know how Satan's system works and be on guard against it. Satan is after the church. He doesn't have to worry about the unbelievers because he already has them. But he will try to lead you and me either into false doctrine or false living. With that in mind, I want to leave you with a few things to think about and apply.

Lesson number one: Just because something is a miracle, that doesn't automatically mean it is from God. He can break through with miracles any time He chooses, but the enemy can work wonders too. So never start with the miracle. Start with the source.

Lesson number two: Objective truth must always take precedence over personal experience. People are always saying, "Well, this is what happened to me." But what happened to you or me is not the standard of what's true. There is nothing wrong with experiencing God, but everything is wrong with an experience that does not align with the truth of Scripture. Our experiences have to rest on the standard of God's revelation to be valid.

Lesson number three: Satan's stuff always looks like the real thing at first. He can disguise himself as an angel of light (2 Cor. 11:14).

But shine the light of God's truth on Satan, and you'll see the horns and pitchfork.

Lesson number four: The farther we drift from God, the closer we are to being deceived by the devil. There is no neutral territory, no demilitarized zone, in spiritual warfare. You're either moving closer to God or sliding closer to Satan.

Lesson number five: When people insist on believing a lie, God will give them all the lies they can handle (2 Thess. 2:11). When people reject His Word, God will make it easier for them to be deceived.

Lesson number six: If you are wrong about the person and work of Jesus, you are wrong—period. The Antichrist is the ultimate denial of every truth about Christ.

Lesson number seven: Satan is out for your destruction, but he can't handle the blood of Jesus Christ. So keep your life under the blood of Jesus; stay close to Christ at all costs.

9

PROPHECY AND THE TRIBULATION

I should have put the notice "to be continued" at the end of the previous chapter, because this is really part two of our study on the tribulation period.

I couldn't talk about the Antichrist, the major figure of the tribulation, without covering some of the events that will take place during these seven years. So with that background, I want to take another brief overview of this prophetic time when the wrath of God falls on rebellious man.

When you realize that most of the book of Revelation is devoted to the tribulation, it becomes obvious that all we can do here is survey some of the highlights and give you an overview of God's prophetic plan as it unfolds. That's what I want to do in this chapter.

Images of the Tribulation

The tribulation was prophesied in the Old Testament, particularly in its impact upon Israel. Jeremiah says it is a time of "terror" and "dread," and compares the pain to a woman in labor. No wonder the prophet says this period will be "the time of Jacob's distress" (Jer. 30:5–7). In the second three-and-a-half years, the Antichrist will unleash his fury on Israel.

Jesus also used the imagery of birth pains in His classic teaching on the tribulation (Matt. 24:4–28). The early warning signs include "wars and rumors of wars," along with "famines and earthquakes" (vv. 6–7). Then Jesus said, "But all these things are merely the beginning of birth pangs" (v. 8). This is the first half of the seven-year period.

The Lord's reference to "the abomination of desolation" (v. 15) marks the start of "great tribulation" (v. 21). We know this to be the midpoint of the tribulation, when the Antichrist crushes apostate religion and sets up his image in the rebuilt Jerusalem temple, demanding to be worshiped as God.

Any woman delivering a child knows that the earliest labor pangs are only the beginning of the painful birth process. The pain usually intensifies as the moment of birth draws near. That's what it will be like on earth in the tribulation, as God's wrath against a sinful world comes to full birth.

If you have ever wondered why sinful man is allowed to do certain things, and why sin is permitted to run its course, it's because God has given mankind some limited autonomy. But that comes to an end when the tribulation begins. It is the Lord's day from beginning to end, not man's.

With these images in mind, let's continue our survey of this horrific period of God's judgment called the tribulation.

CONDITIONS IN THE TRIBULATION

In the previous chapter, I mentioned the fact that the tribulation will actually begin peacefully for those on earth. After giving us the comforting word that the church will be caught away by the Lord (1 Thess. 4:13–18), Paul continued: "The day of the Lord will come just like a thief in the night. While they are saying, 'Peace and safety!' then destruction will come upon them suddenly like labor pains upon a woman with child, and they will not escape" (5:2–3).

A Time of Deceptive Peace

When the tribulation begins, people will actually be positive. We saw that the main reason for this feeling of security is that the Antichrist will come as a champion of peace and solve the unsolvable conflict in the Middle East.

But there may be other reasons for a deceptive sense of well-being. It could be that the stock market will be hitting all-time highs. It's also possible that as the tribulation begins, there will be no major wars.

Remember, the world won't know who the Antichrist really is when he appears on the scene. Even though the church will be gone, life will continue, as is obvious from chapters 4–18 of Revelation. These chapters describe the judgments of the tribulation on those left on earth, and Revelation 17–18 in particular show that commercial and even religious life will have carried on after the rapture.

There will also be a sense of euphoria in Israel in the first half of the tribulation. The Antichrist's covenant will allow for the rebuilding of the temple in Jerusalem and the resumption of the sacrificial system. So the Jews will have their temple and their worship restored.

The Outpouring of God's Work

The time of tribulation is referred to in both the Old and New Testaments as "the day of the Lord" (cf. Isaiah 13:6; 1 Thess. 5:2). This period is the opposite of the day of man, which is in effect today and during which God's grace limits the full expression of His wrath. But when the day of the Lord comes, there will be no holding back His judgment.

Then the world's false sense of peace is going to end as suddenly as a pregnant woman being stabbed awake in the middle of the night by her first labor pain. The outpouring of God's judgment on earth during the tribulation begins in Revelation 6 with the breaking of a seal. This is the first of seven seals, followed by seven trumpets and then seven bowls—overlapping judgments that contain the fullness of God's wrath against sin.

You can read Revelation 6–18 for yourself and see how the horror of the tribulation builds until Jesus returns to defeat the Antichrist (Rev. 19:11–21). John begins in Revelation 6, "I saw when the Lamb broke one of the seven seals, and I heard one of the four living creatures saying as with a voice of thunder, 'Come.' I looked, and behold, a white horse, and he who sat on it had a bow; and a crown was given to him, and he went out conquering and to conquer" (vv. 1–2).

The rider going forth on the white horse is Jesus Christ leaving heaven to begin the process of delivering God's wrath and conquering rebellious mankind. I believe the rapture also occurs at this moment, as Christ comes to deliver God's judgment on the earth. The church is called up to meet the Lord in the air as "the day of the Lord" begins.

This rider has a bow, which can be used for long-range warfare. This fits with the picture of the rapture, in which Christ comes not to the earth, as He does at the end of the tribulation, but in the air to call His people home. So He fights Satan long-range, so to speak, from His position in the heavenly places.

You can see the contrast here with the Lord's second coming, because in Revelation 19:15 He comes with a sharp sword for closeup battle. The first seal is really preliminary to the outbreak of chaos in the tribulation. But the opening of the second seal (Rev. 6:3–4) brings the Antichrist on the scene, the one to whom "it was granted to take peace from the earth." Notice that he carries a sword because this is going to be a time of furious conflict, with death on a massive scale.

From this point on, the story is one of total destruction and chaos, all the way to the end of the tribulation. Conditions just continue to get worse. The fourth seal, for example, destroys one-fourth of the world's population. That will be several billion people. We can't even imagine death on this kind of scale.

The Antichrist is going to march on Israel during this time (Dan. 11:40–45), striking out at nations such as Egypt on his way to the "Beautiful Land" (v. 41). Then Israel will become his command post and the center of the world's activities. The second half of the tribulation is a horrific time, the likes of which the world has never seen.

SALVATION IN THE TRIBULATION

Despite all the judgment and destruction and horror being unleashed on the earth, God will not leave Himself without a witness during the tribulation.

In fact, the world is going to witness the greatest "evangelistic campaign" in history right in the middle of this mess. Masses of people will be saved during the tribulation, but it won't be easy because they will have to accept Christ in the day of His wrath rather than in the day of His grace. And they will face the fury of the Antichrist for their commitment to Christ.

God's Two Witnesses

Even though the Holy Spirit and the church will be gone, God will send two special witnesses to the earth during the tribulation. We're introduced to these two figures in Revelation 11: "I will grant authority to my two witnesses, and they will prophesy for twelve hundred and sixty days, clothed in sackcloth" (v. 3). These men have supernatural powers. They can kill anyone who tries to hurt them with fire from their mouths, and they can stop the rain, turn the waters into blood, and strike the earth with plagues (vv. 5–6).

This description of their powers will sound familiar if you know your Bible. Elijah stopped the rain in Israel for three-and-a-half years, and Moses brought the plagues on Egypt. Interestingly, both Moses and Elijah also appeared with Jesus at His transfiguration (Matt. 17:3).

In other words, these men have unique ministries to fulfill even after their departure from earth. Elijah was raptured to heaven in a chariot of fire, and Moses' body was buried by God so that no one knows where it is. The evidence suggests that the two witnesses of Revelation 11 are Moses and Elijah.

The content of their witness is not specified, but the miracles Moses and Elijah did were testimonies to the true God in the midst of paganism. That may be the type of witness they will bear in the tribulation, pointing people to the true God who is still willing to save.

When the two witnesses have finished their ministry, they will be overcome and killed by the Antichrist. The world will see their dead bodies lying in the streets of Jerusalem and throw a party (Rev. 11:7–10).

People used to wonder how the whole world would be able to see this event and rejoice in the death of these two who were a headache and a torment. But that's not a problem anymore. The two witnesses will be on worldwide stage twenty-four hours a day, because what these guys will do is news. With the onset of live-streaming and social media, the technology to allow this is already in place.

But after three-and-a-half days of lying dead in Jerusalem, the witnesses will be miraculously raised from the dead and raptured to heaven. And the footage will be captured as these two suddenly stand up on their feet.

These two men aren't God's only tribulation witnesses. The Bible says that 144,000 Jewish men will be saved and sealed and become God's witnesses. We need to understand the identity and ministry of this often-misunderstood group.

The 144,000 Jews

The 144,000 are introduced in Revelation 7:1–8. They are called "the bondservants of our God," and they are clearly Jewish (vv. 3–4). And later, they are said to be male virgins, specially consecrated to

God, and blameless (Rev. 14:4–5). Besides, they aren't even chosen until the tribulation.

Now that should be enough information to eliminate a lot of misguided teaching about the 144,000. You don't need to join a group and go knocking on doors to try and make yourself worthy to be in this group. You probably don't qualify, and neither do I.

These witnesses will be converted during the first half of the tribulation, and they will serve as evangelists for the gospel during this time. They are the "first fruits" (Rev. 14:4) of many other Jews who will be saved by the time the tribulation ends.

So the gospel is going to be preached to the whole world during the tribulation, and everybody on earth will hear the message because everything these witnesses say and do will be broadcast through the convenience of digital media. Their ministry will lead to a great multitude of Gentiles being saved during the tribulation—a number so large no one can count it (Rev. 7:9; cf. v. 14). The cost in suffering for following Christ will be tremendous, but many will choose Him over allegiance to the Antichrist.

THE OUTBREAK OF THE TRIBULATION

As the tribulation approaches its midpoint, there comes an escalation of judgments and chaos and warfare as events move toward the final half, "the time of Jacob's distress."

Satan's Defeat and Attack on Israel

Israel's distress in the tribulation is obvious from the opening scene of Revelation 12:

> A great sign appeared in heaven: a woman clothed with the
> sun, and the moon under her feet, and on her head a crown of

twelve stars; and she was with child; and she cried out, being in labor and in pain to give birth.

Then another sign appeared in heaven: and behold, a great red dragon having seven heads and ten horns, and on his heads were seven diadems. And his tail swept away a third of the stars of heaven and threw them to the earth. And the dragon stood before the woman who was about to give birth, so that when she gave birth he might devour her child. (vv. 1–4)

The woman in this vision represents Israel, who gave birth to Jesus Christ. And there is no mistaking the identity of the Dragon. This is Satan trying to destroy Christ, the offspring of Israel. Satan knows that if he can kill God's Redeemer and King, there will be no kingdom. But that attempt failed (v. 5).

So Satan escalates the war, and what follows is war in heaven between Satan and the archangel Michael and their forces. Satan is defeated and thrown down to the earth (vv. 7–9), where he will operate directly for the remainder of the tribulation in the physical realm. Satan's banishment from heaven marks the beginning of the great tribulation.

That alone is going to make things much worse on earth. To get to you and me today, Satan has to go through God. But in the great tribulation, Satan will run the show directly from the earth, and anyone who wants to come to Christ will have to take on the devil and his persecution directly.

After Satan is thrown down to the earth, he will be unhindered in his operation against the earth dwellers. And he will have "great wrath" (Rev. 12:12), which he will vent on Israel. This will be the devil's last chance to defeat God by destroying Israel, so he is going to pull out all the stops.

Satan will persecute the woman, Israel, "pour[ing] water like a river out of his mouth after the woman" to sweep her away (vv. 13–16).

Those Israelites who flee (vv. 6, 16) will be protected by God, but those who stay will come under Satan's attack. That's why Jesus warned His listeners to flee Jerusalem immediately, not stopping for anything, when they saw the abomination of desolation in the temple (Matt. 24:15–18).

The Antichrist's "Fatal Wound"

This brings us back pretty much full circle to where we began in the previous chapter, the appearance of the Antichrist in Revelation 13. We presented a lot of information about the Antichrist's person and program, but we haven't dealt with his fatal wound. "I saw one of his heads as if it had been slain, and his fatal wound was healed. And the whole earth was amazed and followed after the beast" (Rev. 13:3).

We don't know for sure what this wound is a reference to, but apparently the Beast is going to receive a deathblow and then be brought back to life by Satan as a miracle to further deceive the world. And it will work. By this time God is going to help people be deceived who insist on being deceived (see 2 Thess. 2:10–12).

The Antichrist will gradually assume power by bringing peace to the Middle East and building up apostate religion. But if anyone is reluctant to believe him or hand over the reins of world power to him, his resurrection will make a tremendous impression. People are going to listen to someone who can get up out of the grave. Satan even counterfeits Christ's resurrection by bringing his false Christ back to life.

The Antichrist's Allies

As we saw previously, the Antichrist is going to have some powerful allies. First, he will be empowered by Satan (Rev. 13:4–7). He will also be assisted by the False Prophet, whom we have discussed (vv. 11–18) and who has some awesome satanic powers of his own in his ability to perform miracles. Together, Satan, the Antichrist, and the False Prophet form the satanic trinity in imitation of the triune God.

When we see these three in action, we are reminded of the absolute importance of knowing and believing the truth, so we won't fall victim to the lies of Satan. The False Prophet isn't the only one in the tribulation who will perform miraculous signs. So will God's two witnesses, but most of the world won't believe them because people will have allowed themselves to be deluded by Satan's lies. Refuse to believe the truth, and you are a sitting duck for lies.

The Antichrist also has plenty of human beings who will be more than willing to align themselves with him. We reviewed the fact that he will acquire religious control, becoming the leader of the apostate church by encrusting it with jewels and gold and all sorts of wealth (Rev. 17:1–4). Organized religion will do the Antichrist's will, until such time as he turns on this false system and destroys it.

He will also accumulate enormous political power. He will be in charge of ten kings, the reunited Roman Empire, who "receive authority as kings with the beast for one hour. These have one purpose, and they give their power and authority to the beast" (Rev. 17:12–13).

In other words, Europe will say to the Antichrist, "We will follow you wherever you want us to go." And he will say like Adolf Hitler, "Today Europe, tomorrow the world." The Antichrist wants to be a world ruler, not just a European ruler.

We also dealt with the Antichrist's total economic control, which he will ultimately exercise through the mark he will force upon anyone who hopes to carry out even normal everyday transactions (Rev. 13:16–18). Whoever doesn't accept the 666 mark will starve. The problem is that anyone who accepts the Antichrist's mark and confirms allegiance to him will be judged and condemned by God (Rev. 14:9–11).

The Response of Stubborn Unbelief

I want to wrap up our study of the tribulation by looking at one more amazing fact. You might think that when all the horrors prophesied in the Bible begin unfolding on earth, people would run to God crying for mercy and salvation. You'd think that once people realize they are in the last days of God's judgment and they see all these terrifying things unfolding before their eyes, they would repent and beg God's forgiveness.

Not so. According to Revelation 9:20–21a, "The rest of mankind, who were not killed by these plagues, did not repent of the works of their hands, so as not to worship demons, and the idols of gold and of silver and of brass and of stone and of wood, which can neither see nor hear nor walk . . . they did not repent."

Then in Revelation 16:9 we read, "Men were scorched with fierce heat; and they blasphemed the name of God who has the power over these plagues, and they did not repent so as to give Him glory" (see also v. 11).

God is warning the world today to repent and flee His wrath to come. The day of His grace is still upon us, and whoever wishes may come to the cross and find forgiveness. But when the day of God's judgment falls, sinners will not be inclined to seek forgiveness. That's why witnessing about Christ's salvation now while we have time is so important. As kingdom followers of Jesus Christ, now is the time to share the love and truth of His gospel.

10

PROPHECY AND THE BATTLE OF ARMAGEDDON

Since God never leaves anything undone or half-finished, we can be sure that He will not leave any loose ends in bringing the great tribulation to a close. In fact, this period during which Satan has been in command and evil has run rampant will end with the devil's most foolish move of all. It's an all-out attempt to use his evil forces to defeat Jesus Christ and the armies of heaven in head-on combat. The Bible says this awesome, climactic battle will occur in "the place which in Hebrew is called Har-Magedon" (Rev. 16:16). We know this as the Battle of Armageddon, the time when God's wrath against sin and sinners will be unleashed and the Antichrist's reign in the great tribulation will be ended.

The world has been interested in the subject of Armageddon for a long time because a lot of people believe that the next global war will be so cataclysmic it will be history's final conflict. Some think it will be a nuclear holocaust that will annihilate mankind.

Since we take our information from God's Word rather than from man's ideas or news headlines, we are going to look at what the Bible teaches about the Battle of Armageddon. In this chapter we will focus on the preparation for the battle, and in the next chapter we will see how this great conflict ends.

The Hill of Megiddo overlooks the massive plain of the Valley of Jezreel, an area that extends for miles. The ancient city of Megiddo lay on the strategic north-south trade route between Mesopotamia and Egypt, and therefore it came to be important militarily.

This will be the staging area and command center for a series of conflicts that make up the Battle of Armageddon—the war to end all wars, prophetically speaking. Revelation 16 briefly describes the preparations for the conflict, and then in Revelation 19 we see Jesus riding out of heaven to engage the devil, the Antichrist, and the False Prophet, Satan's unholy trinity.

Preparing for Armageddon

Preparations for Armageddon begin as the angel pours out the sixth bowl of God's judgment on the earth (Rev. 16:12–16). God's wrath on the unbelieving world during the great tribulation will be executed in a series of judgments that include seals, trumpets, and then bowls.

There are seven bowls altogether, so at this point we are near the end of the tribulation. John wrote:

> The sixth angel poured out his bowl upon the great river, the Euphrates; and its water was dried up, so that the way would be prepared for the kings from the east.
>
> And I saw coming out of the mouth of the dragon and out of the mouth of the beast and out of the mouth of the false prophet, three unclean spirits like frogs; for they are spirits of demons, performing signs, which go out to the kings of the

whole world, to gather them together for the war of the great day of God, the Almighty. (vv. 12–14)

When the time comes for Armageddon, the great Euphrates River is going to be turned into a wading pool so the armies of Eastern powers can come to Israel to wage war against God.

The Reason for the Battle

The first thing I want you to see is the reason for this battle. This is a battle inspired by the false trinity to overthrow the true Trinity. The demons that call the kings to battle come from each member of this unholy trio.

This is all-out, desperate war against God and His Son (Rev. 19:19). Armageddon is the climax of the angelic conflict that began in heaven, was transferred to earth, and now has come full circle as Satan tries to defeat God by force.

Armageddon is also the world's final response to God's call for repentance. Throughout the tribulation, God will be calling on mankind to repent. But most will refuse (Rev. 16:9, 11) and align themselves with the Antichrist, with the result that God will allow Satan to gather together the world's armies for God's swift judgment.

It won't surprise you to learn that Armageddon was prophesied in the Old Testament. Joel 3:9–17 is one of those passages, in which the place of battle is called "the valley of decision" (v. 14). The prophet used that term because this is the place where unbelieving men will make their decision to join Satan in making war against God.

Earlier in the tribulation, many people will make a decision for Satan when they accept the number 666, the mark of the Beast. That number will enable them to buy and sell. So that decision will be motivated by the desire to eat and stay alive. But the choice to join Satan at Armageddon is a deliberate attempt to defeat God.

Armageddon is also prophesied in Psalm 2, where we read that the nations are in an uproar, devising "a vain thing" (v. 1). What is this futile plan? They decide to take their stand against God and against Jesus Christ, and say, "Let us tear their fetters apart, and cast away their cords from us!" (v. 3). God's response is to scoff at their rebellion (v. 4).

Satan's Attempt to Destroy Israel

The key to Armageddon is Satan's attempt to defeat God by destroying Israel (Rev. 12:13–17). The battle takes place in the Holy Land, with the focus on Jerusalem. This is because even though Satan knows it is futile to wage war against God because the outcome was decided at the cross, he believes that if he could eradicate Israel, he would destroy God's covenant promises. That would make God a liar.

God made covenants with Israel to give them their land, to redeem them, to bless them, and to give them an eternal King through David's line. Some of these promises were fulfilled with Christ's first coming, and the rest of them will be fulfilled when Christ returns to take the throne of David.

Satan can't get at God directly, so he will go after God's people. That's why he wants Israel, and that's why Israel will never know real peace until Jesus Christ sits on the throne of David. The devil will always keep some nation or group stirred up to come against Israel. Trying to stop God's plan for Israel is not a new strategy for Satan. When Jesus was born as Israel's Messiah, Satan filled King Herod's evil heart with a plan to murder all the baby boys under two years old who lived in or near Bethlehem (Matt. 2:16).

When that didn't work, Satan moved Israel to reject and crucify its Messiah. But the resurrection of Jesus Christ overcame that strategy, so Satan has had to come at Israel from other directions.

The destruction of Jerusalem and the dispersion of the Israelites in AD 70 must have seemed like another high point for the devil.

Israel ceased to exist as a nation for almost two thousand years. But in May 1948, God raised Israel out of the ashes of history. The rebirth of Israel was a big setback for Satan, but he is far from finished.

In Revelation 12:1–6, John described Satan's attempt to devour Israel's "child," Jesus Christ, at His birth (v. 4). But since that failed, the devil will unleash intense persecution on Israel for "one thousand two hundred and sixty days" (v. 6), the last three-and-a-half years of the tribulation (see also Rev. 12:13–17). By protecting Israel, God is also protecting His covenant promises.

THE DETAILS OF ARMAGEDDON

Let's focus in a little closer on the details of Armageddon, particularly the armies that will be arrayed against Jesus Christ and the armies of heaven.

An Islamic Invasion

Here's something you may not have seen before, but one of the battles that will lead into Armageddon is an Islamic invasion of Israel. The Middle East is a tinderbox because of the conflict between the Jews and Muslims, and one reason for the ongoing tension is the Muslim mosque that sits directly on the site in Jerusalem where the Jewish temple stood.

The reason it will become so critical is that the Bible indicates the Jews will resume their sacrificial system during the tribulation. If the Antichrist somehow aids the Jews in restoring their temple and sacrifices, that will cause an incredible amount of tension, leading to open warfare.

The invasion of Israel by an Islamic army is prophesied in Ezekiel 38–39. The prophet used the language, descriptions, and place names of his day to explain this coming battle. Ezekiel said in chapter 38:

Son of man, set your face toward Gog of the land of Magog, the prince of Rosh, Meshech and Tubal, and prophesy against him, and say, "Thus says the Lord God . . . I will turn you about and put hooks into your jaws, and I will bring you out, and all your army, horses and horsemen, all of them splendidly attired, a great company with buckler and shield, all of them wielding swords; Persia, Ethiopia and Put with them, all of them with shield and helmet; Gomer with all its troops; Beth-togarmah from the remote parts of the north with all its troops—many peoples with you." (vv. 2–6)

And, furthermore,

"You will come from your place out of the remote parts of the north, you and many peoples with you, all of them riding on horses, a great assembly and a mighty army; and you will come up against My people Israel like a cloud to cover the land." (vv. 15–16a)

God says He is going to be in charge of this program. The demons who will go out of the mouths of the satanic trinity to lure the kings to battle will be used by the Lord as hooks in the mouths of these kings to pull them toward their judgment at Armageddon. God states His purpose: "When I am sanctified through you" (v. 16). The world is going to see God vindicate His righteousness by judging these invaders.

Let's line up the major nations that will be part of this invasion from the Islamic world. Gog was probably a ruler over the land of Magog, which is part of modern-day Turkey. Meshech and Tubal were also part of Asia Minor. Persia is modern-day Iran, Ethiopia is actually part of modern-day Sudan, and Put is Libya. Gomer and Beth-togarmah are also part of Turkey today.

The Iranians are Persians, not Arabs, but all of these areas have one thing in common: the Islamic religion, which is firmly entrenched against Judaism. When the time comes for Armageddon, Satan will use Islamic hostility toward Israel as a pawn in his rebellion against God and his desire to destroy Israel. But God will work above it all to accomplish His prophetic purpose.

God's Intervention

Today's heightened tensions and escalated battles in the Middle East are simply the precursor to this massive invasion that will take place in the end times. Peace efforts between Israel and its neighbors may slow the pace of the hostilities or delay the outbreak of open conflict, but at Armageddon the Islamic nations will see the chance they've always wanted to annihilate Israel.

But God will intervene in a decisive way:

> "My fury will mount up in My anger. . . . I will call for a sword against him on all My mountains. . . . Every man's sword will be against his brother. I will magnify Myself, sanctify Myself, and make Myself known in the sight of many nations; and they will know that I am the LORD." (Ezek. 38:18, 21, 23)

Verses 20 and 22 refer to an earthquake, hailstones, fire, and brimstone that God will rain down on the invaders. So when this massive Islamic coalition comes against Israel, God will use natural phenomena to wipe them out. The slaughter will be so great that Revelation 14:20 refers to the blood running several feet deep for several hundred miles as God supernaturally imposes Himself on this battle.

Israel's Repentance

The Battle of Armageddon will accomplish another objective besides the destruction of God's enemies. It will be the beginning of

Israel's repentance and spiritual awakening. Speaking of the events of Armageddon, God said in Ezekiel 39:22, "And the house of Israel will know that I am the LORD their God from that day onward."

Remember that Israel will welcome the Antichrist in the first half of the tribulation because he will be the great peacemaker in the Middle East. He will appear to be Israel's friend and protector, and the nation will be allowed to rebuild its temple and reinstitute the Mosaic sacrifices.

But when the Antichrist turns on Israel in his fury, the nation will undergo intense persecution. When God reveals Himself at Armageddon, the Jews will see that the Lord God alone is their God.

A PROPHETIC POINTER TO ARMAGEDDON

Another important nation in the Middle East also hates Israel. This is the kingdom of Iraq, and it deserves special attention from a prophetic standpoint because what has happened in Iraq is a precursor to the Battle of Armageddon. Iraq is a pointer to Armageddon.

The "Great Harlot"

In Revelation 17 and 18, we meet "the great harlot" (17:1), which John described as "a woman sitting on a scarlet beast, full of blasphemous names, having seven heads and ten horns" (v. 3). We're told the identity of this harlot: "On her forehead a name was written, a mystery, 'Babylon the Great, the mother of harlots and of the abominations of the earth'" (v. 5).

This is a very influential place. John later said of Babylon, "The woman whom you saw is the great city, which reigns over the kings of the earth" (v. 18).

This Babylon is called a mystery, which in the Bible is something that wasn't known before but is now being revealed. The Babylon of

Revelation 17 and 18 is a mystery because it is Babylon appearing in a new form.

Of course, Babylon was a major city in Old Testament times, beginning as Babel where mankind rebelled against God (Gen. 11:1–9). Probably the greatest king in the Old Testament was Nebuchadnezzar, the king of Babylon.

According to nonbiblical sources, Babylon also became the center of mystery religions and secret pagan rites that survived after the ancient city itself was destroyed. So Babylon came to symbolize false religion and idolatry as opposed to the worship of the true God. In the Revelation, Babylon comes up before God for its final judgment.

Babylon Restored

The groundwork for that future judgment began to be laid when huge investments to restore the city were made by Saddam Hussein. He attempted to rebuild on its ancient site, which just happens to be about fifty miles south of Baghdad in modern-day Iraq. He even called himself the new Nebuchadnezzar. Since that time, though, it has largely sat untouched. However, efforts to restore the legacy of the city have recently started taking place. In 2019, the UNESCO World Heritage Convention named the historic city of Babylon a World Heritage Site.

Revelation 18 indicates that the rebuilt Babylon will be a great commercial as well as religious center. Not only will it be a wealthy city (v. 11), but it will make the nations of the world wealthy too (v. 19). When Babylon falls under God's judgment, the merchants of earth, "who became rich from her," will mourn over her destruction (Rev. 18:15–19).

What does Iraq have that can make the merchants of earth rich? Oil! The Middle East's oil reserves not only make that region rich, but they enrich anyone who deals with them, because the whole world is dependent upon oil.

Armageddon could be triggered by an oil crisis, which would draw the armies of the earth to the Middle East. Babylon is going to rise again, and the Middle East conflict and the oil situation could be setting the stage for Armageddon.

Restored Babylon Destroyed

But evidently, Babylon itself will not be around for Armageddon. The apostle John saw the harlot Babylon riding a scarlet-colored beast (Rev. 17:3), which means she is being supported by the Antichrist. But then the Beast and his kings turn on the harlot and destroy her when the Antichrist takes absolute control (vv. 16–17).

Why will the Antichrist destroy Babylon? Because, as we saw above, it will be the center of a false religious system as well as a commercial center. The Antichrist needs to destroy false religion as a prelude to setting himself up as God and demanding to be worshiped.

The Antichrist also needs to control the oil fields to control global commerce, so Babylon is going to become an obstacle that the Beast needs to rid himself of. He will already control Europe and its union at this point, which as we said earlier could include the United States.

But whoever controls the oil, whether output or reserves, controls global wealth, so the Antichrist will go after the oil. The stage is being set for the prophecies of Revelation 17 and 18 to be fulfilled, clearing the way for the great conflict of Armageddon.

So Babylon will fall in a great judgment just prior to the Battle of Armageddon. The Antichrist will support and use Babylon as a stepping-stone to his worldwide power. Babylon will be useful to him for a while because of its oil reserves and also because of its hostility to Israel. Remember, Armageddon will be Satan's last-ditch effort to destroy the Jews.

SUMMONING THE NATIONS TO ARMAGEDDON

We're now back to our starting point in Revelation 16:12–16, when the demons draw the kings of the earth to Megiddo, or the Valley of Jezreel. These kings will have no allegiance to God, so they will readily come under demonic influence.

The numbers here are staggering. Megiddo is an area two hundred miles long, so it will have no problem accommodating the leaders of the armies that will mass for Armageddon. Revelation 9:16 pictures an army of two hundred million mounted troops. Joel prophesied the Battle of Armageddon as the biggest bloodbath in human history (Joel 3:9–17).

Let me show you who's coming to this battle. We know that the European alliance is going to be there because the Antichrist will be over the ten nations of Europe. The "kings of the east" will also come because the Euphrates River will be dried up to make it possible for them to cross and attack Israel (Rev. 16:12).

Euphrates is a seventeen-hundred-mile river that runs from Turkey all the way down to the Persian Gulf. On the east side of the Euphrates is China, which could easily assemble an army of two hundred million mounted troops all by itself.

We'll see in the next chapter that the Battle of Armageddon isn't much of a battle at all. Revelation 19 says a sword will come out of Christ's mouth, the spoken Word of God, and annihilate all the armies gathered to oppose Him. Satan and his forces will be totally and swiftly defeated, and the battlefield will become a feeding ground for birds. Armageddon will be a horrible day of slaughter, worse than anything we could imagine.

11

PROPHECY AND THE KING'S RETURN FOR THE MILLENNIAL REIGN

One of the most famous moments in World War II occurred early in the war when the Japanese army stormed the Philippines and forced United States General Douglas MacArthur to leave the islands. MacArthur left the Philippines, but not before issuing his famous promise, "I shall return." And he did, walking ashore at Leyte in the Philippines several years later as a victorious general.

MacArthur wasn't the first leader to promise his own return. Jesus Christ said, "I will come again" (John 14:3), and the angels who appeared at His ascension told the disciples, "This Jesus, who has been taken up from you into heaven, will come in just the same way as you have watched Him go into heaven" (Acts 1:11).

Christ's return to earth is the climax of history and the event anticipated in so much of Bible prophecy. Jesus Christ will return at the end of the great tribulation, the last half of Daniel's seventieth week, to conquer His enemies and usher in His thousand-year millennial kingdom. The chronology of events is laid out for us in Revelation 19:11–21.

These verses describe the climax of Satan's rebellion, and his defeat, at the Battle of Armageddon. We will consider this important event, but I also want to study another judgment that will take place when Christ returns—the often-confusing judgment Jesus outlined in Matthew 25:31–46.

THE PURPOSES OF CHRIST'S COMING

The second coming of Jesus Christ is initiated with this brief but powerful word from the apostle John: "I saw heaven opened" (Rev. 19:11). This announcement signals Christ's return to earth to accomplish God's purposes for Satan and his allies, and for His chosen nation Israel, at Armageddon. The second coming will also fulfill mankind's destiny in God's plan as He reverses the curse of sin and ends the angelic conflict that began with Satan's rebellion in heaven. Let's see how these purposes will be brought about when heaven opens and Christ rides forth.

The Gathering at Armageddon

The Greek general Alexander the Great is reported to have said that Megiddo, the scene for the Battle of Armageddon, is the most natural battlefield in the world.

Alexander was talking about a plain that stretches for many miles and allows for the movement of vast armies. It's here that Satan, the Antichrist, and the False Prophet will gather their armies for a last stand against God that will accomplish His purpose of judgment against them.

When heaven opened, John saw an awesome sight. "Behold, a white horse, and He who sat on it is called Faithful and True, and in righteousness He judges and wages war" (Rev. 19:11).

The image of a conqueror riding a white horse was something that anybody in New Testament times could have readily related to. When a victorious Roman general returned from battle with his captives and the spoils, he rode through Rome in a victory parade on a white horse. A white horse was a symbol of victory in that day. So the Bible pictures Jesus Christ as returning to earth for His day of conquest, the day when He lays claim to the ultimate and final victory in history. In Zechariah 14:2 the Lord says, "I will gather all the nations against Jerusalem to battle." We saw in the previous chapter that, according to Revelation 16:12–14, Satan and his unholy trinity draw the nations together to do battle at Armageddon.

The difference is that Zechariah was speaking from God's viewpoint, while John was describing events from the viewpoint of earth. My point is that even when Satan is doing his stuff, he is actually accomplishing God's program. On Satan's best day, he is helping achieve the program of God. Don't ever forget that.

God's Defense of Israel

Let's go back to Zechariah 14, which describes Satan's attempt to destroy Israel at Armageddon and God's defense of His people:

> I will gather all the nations against Jerusalem to battle, and the city will be captured, the houses plundered, the women ravished and half of the city exiled, but the rest of the people will not be cut off from the city. Then the LORD will go forth and fight against those nations, as when He fights on a day of battle. In that day His feet will stand on the Mount of Olives, which is in front of Jerusalem on the east; and the Mount of Olives will be split in its middle from east to west by a very large valley, so that half of the mountain will move toward the north and the other half toward the south. (vv. 2–4)

We know that God is going to intervene supernaturally at Armageddon, and this prophecy gives us more of the details. The Mount of Olives is situated right in front of Jerusalem, not far from the city. I've stood there myself and taught from that location when we were filming the documentary Bible study *Journey with Jesus*. It's an awe-inspiring location. Jesus Christ ascended from this location on the Mount of Olives, called "Olivet" in Acts 1:12, and He will return to that spot to defend His people as the battle rages against Jerusalem—the focal point of Armageddon.

It's clear from these verses in Zechariah that at one point in the conflict, things will be looking horrible for Jerusalem. Satan has always been intent on destroying God's people, and at that point in time he will be making the most of his chance.

But things are going to change when Jesus' feet touch down on the Mount of Olives. The mountain will divide all the way down to the Dead Sea. In fact, Ezekiel 47:1–10 says when this happens, the Dead Sea will become a place of life instead of a place where nothing can live because of the salt content. Nature itself will respond and come alive at the return of Christ (see Rom. 8:19–22).

When Jesus Christ comes back as Israel's Defender at Armageddon, the tide of battle will suddenly change. Zechariah 12:2–4 describes this:

> Behold, I am going to make Jerusalem a cup that causes reeling to all the peoples around; and when the siege is against Jerusalem, it will also be against Judah. It will come about in that day that I will make Jerusalem a heavy stone for all the peoples; all who lift it will be severely injured. And all the nations of the earth will be gathered against it. "In that day," declares the LORD, "I will strike every horse with bewilderment and his rider with madness. But I will watch over the house of Judah."

When Jesus enters the battle, things will change in a hurry. This prophecy is very graphic in describing the injury that Israel will inflict on its attackers when the Lord comes to strengthen His people and fight for them.

I love the way Zechariah describes the way God will empower Israel against its enemies. "In that day the LORD will defend the inhabitants of Jerusalem, and the one who is feeble among them in that day will be like David, and the house of David will be like God, like the angel of the LORD before them" (Zech. 12:8).

If you have ever wondered why no one can destroy Israel, even though it sits as a tiny nation surrounded and outnumbered by its enemies, here is the reason: God is Israel's Defender.

Fulfilling Mankind's Destiny

Here is another, and broader, purpose that Christ will accomplish at His return. What I mean here is that Christ's return and victory over Satan will be the culmination of the reason for which mankind was created in the first place. This takes us all the way back to the beginning of our studies, to the angelic conflict that began in heaven.

God created man as a lesser being than the angels to demonstrate His power to Satan and all the angels who followed him in rebellion (Gen. 1:26–28; Ps. 8:3–6). God said to Satan, in effect, "I am going to defeat you through a man" (Dan. 7:13–14; Heb. 2:5–8, 14).

So Satan went after Adam and Eve, and he figured he had checkmated God when Adam fell. But God promised a coming Seed, another man named Jesus Christ, the last Adam, through whom God would ultimately triumph. Satan didn't count on God becoming a man in the person of Christ.

Satan went after Christ too, first at His birth and then on the cross, but to no avail. Now, at Armageddon, we see Jesus and redeemed mankind in the armies of heaven coming to administer Satan's defeat. Jesus

Christ is God's agent of judgment as well as His agent of redemption (see John 5:27).

THE DESCRIPTION OF CHRIST'S SECOND COMING

With all of this as a backdrop, we're ready for Revelation 19 and its magnificent description of Jesus Christ returning in power and glory. This is not the baby of Bethlehem we sing about, or the gentle Jesus who holds children in His lap. This is the God-man of heaven coming to judge and make war.

And what a return it will be. John said that "every eye will see Him" (Rev. 1:7). The return of Jesus Christ will definitely be unlike anything ever seen or experienced before. Notice what the Bible says about Christ as He rides out of heaven.

The Bible says that the One who is coming from heaven on the white horse "is called Faithful and True" (Rev. 19:11). Jesus is called Faithful because as Perfect Man, He is perfectly obedient to the will of God—unlike the first Adam, who failed and plunged the human race into sin. Christ is also called True in contrast to Satan and his cohorts, who are liars. Because He is God, Jesus is the embodiment of truth (see John 14:6). It takes a person like this to judge righteously.

I'm intrigued by the name Jesus carries that "no one knows except Himself" (Rev. 19:12). It is a very powerful thing whenever God gives you a name, because in the Bible names always reflect character. So apparently there is some aspect of Christ's character that is still unrevealed, and something special about Him we are yet to learn. Then in verse 13 we read, "His name is called The Word of God." Jesus Christ is the ultimate expression of God's character and person because He is God in the flesh. There's still another name given to Christ in this passage. "On His robe and on His thigh He has a name written, 'King of kings, and Lord of lords' " (v. 16). Jesus is the King of anybody else called a king and the Lord of anybody else called a lord because all of earth's rulers will bow to Him.

At His return Jesus will also wear "many diadems" (Rev. 19:12). These crowns are emblems of His conquest because He is coming to put down rebellion and take over.

The Lord will also be "clothed with a robe dipped in blood" (v. 13) because He is coming for judgment. There will be no question whatsoever about Jesus' authority or His purpose when He returns to this earth.

What's more, Jesus is not coming back alone. "The armies which are in heaven, clothed in fine linen, white and clean, were following Him on white horses" (Rev. 19:14). These are the saints in heaven, including the church that was raptured at the beginning of the tribulation. That means we're in this army.

These saints are dressed in white linen, which is symbolic of righteousness—in this case, the "righteous acts of the saints" (v. 8). Why are we in righteous dress? Because after the rapture, we will go through the judgment seat of Christ where our unworthy acts will be burned up. Only the good will remain, so when we return with Christ to reign with Him in the kingdom, we will appear in righteous clothing.

Jesus is also not coming back unarmed. "From His mouth comes a sharp sword, so that with it He may strike down the nations, and He will rule them with a rod of iron; and He treads the wine press of the fierce wrath of God, the Almighty" (Rev. 19:15).

The sharp sword in Jesus' mouth is God's Word, which the writer of Hebrews said is capable of discerning the deepest thoughts and motives of our lives (Heb. 4:12). This sword speaks of judgment. So does the imagery of the "wine press" of God's wrath.

Jesus Christ will judge and rule the nations by His Word. So certain is this judgment, in fact, that before the Battle of Armageddon even begins, an angel appears to announce the outcome and invite the birds to "the great supper of God" (Rev. 19:17) at which they will feed on the carcasses of all God's enemies.

Those gathered against God at Armageddon are people who have refused to repent throughout the tribulation, even though God has been demonstrating that He alone is God.

John said, "I saw the beast and the kings of the earth and their armies assembled to make war against Him who sat on the horse and against His army" (v. 19). The armies are massed together for what they think is a great battle during which they will overthrow God. But what they are really gathering for is a great judgment instead.

THE POWER OF CHRIST'S SECOND COMING

With the two sides at Armageddon drawn up against each other, the next thing we see is the lightning-quick, awesome power that Christ displays at His return.

The fact is that Armageddon isn't much of a battle. It's decided very quickly, over almost before it starts. And by the way, Jesus Christ is used to fighting these kinds of quick battles. He fought one as the "angel of the Lord," the way He appeared in the Old Testament before His incarnation. When Jesus Christ strikes in judgment, it is cataclysmic. He doesn't need years or months or even days to dispatch His foes. He simply speaks the Word, and His enemies fall.

There is certain judgment in store for the participants of Armageddon who try to overcome Christ:

> The beast was seized, and with him the false prophet who performed the signs in his presence, by which he deceived those who had received the mark of the beast and those who worshiped his image; these two were thrown alive into the lake of fire which burns with brimstone. And the rest were killed with the sword which came from the mouth of Him who

sat on the horse, and all the birds were filled with their flesh. (Rev. 19:20–21)

Jesus will see to a swift victory at Armageddon, and those there will later face God at the great white throne judgment. But He has swifter judgment in store for the Antichrist and his False Prophet. They will go directly into the lake of fire without even experiencing death.

This is a terrifying picture of judgment, of God's wrath poured out on Satan and on sinful humanity. With two-thirds of the satanic trinity taken care of, Jesus will turn His attention to Satan himself, the ringleader of this rebellion. Armageddon will be followed by the devil's "arrest" and incarceration for one thousand years. This is how John described it:

> Then I saw an angel coming down from heaven, holding the key of the abyss and a great chain in his hand. And he laid hold of the dragon, the serpent of old, who is the devil and Satan, and bound him for a thousand years; and he threw him into the abyss, and shut it and sealed it over him, so that he would not deceive the nations any longer, until the thousand years were completed; after these things he must be released for a short time. (Rev. 20:1–3)

This imprisonment is not Satan's final, eternal doom, because at the end of the millennium he will go out once more to deceive the nations and make his very last stand against Christ. This brief rebellion will also result in Satan's defeat and his being cast into the lake of fire forever (Rev. 20:7–10).

Satan is going to be locked away for a thousand years because that's how long Christ is going to rule in perfect righteousness on earth. The devil's absence is one thing that will make the kingdom so wonderful. Jesus is running the show, and the devil will be nowhere to be found.

During the kingdom we will experience what mankind has always been searching for: a peace on earth with no hatred or war or crime or other visible signs of sin or rebellion. Life in the kingdom will go on naturally, in the sense that people will be born and die and carry on everyday kinds of activities because this is not eternity yet. That's why when Satan rebels one last time at the end of the millennium, he will still be able to find some people who will follow him.

The second coming of Christ will usher the Antichrist and his kingdom off the earth and into hell, and usher in His own thousand-year reign of righteousness.

Israel's Repentance

I also want to review briefly what will happen to Israel at Christ's second coming. Israel will not be included in the judgment of the nations, which is basically a Gentile judgment. According to Ezekiel 20:33–38, God will separate Israel out and enter into judgment personally with His chosen people.

At this time the Israelites will look upon Christ, the One whom they have pierced (Zech. 12:10), and will mourn over Him. Israel will recognize Jesus Christ as its Messiah, and all the years of rejecting Him will end. Christ will sit on David's throne as the acknowledged King of Israel and King of the world.

Some people said for years that end time events and the second coming of Christ sounded too much like a Hollywood script to be true. Too many things had to happen to prepare the world for His coming. But today, those events don't seem so far away. The nation of Israel exists in the midst of its enemies. A European union exists. The means for instantaneous, worldwide communication is available right now. These things are worth noting, but God doesn't call us to look for signs. He calls us to look for the Son. The reason is because it is the Son who will rule in the millennial kingdom.

THE MILLENNIUM

The millennium is the perfect way to end the clock ticking of time as we know it. Only God could have conceived of a program that brings His creation called time to an end in such a way that everything messed up by sin and Satan is restored, God's promises are fulfilled, His righteousness is fully vindicated and displayed, and every legitimate human longing for peace and justice is met. All of that, and more, will come to pass when Jesus Christ establishes His thousand-year kingdom on earth. We call it the "millennium" from the Latin term for the Greek word *chilias*, which means "thousand."

Some people think this is just a symbolic term for time, so that the thousand-year kingdom is not literal but merely a way of speaking about eternity. However, John used this term six times in Revelation 20:1–7 to describe this period that follows the tribulation, and He gave no indication that it is to be taken metaphorically. The millennium is a specific period of time.

There will be no lasting peace until Jesus Himself brings it, and He will do so on His terms. His enemies will be destroyed at Armageddon, Satan will be locked away for a thousand years, and the Antichrist and the False Prophet will be sent to hell. No one will be able to stop Christ from taking over. Let's look at what the Bible says about this glorious period of time.

THE COMPLETENESS OF THE MILLENNIUM

Because the millennium is the completion of time and the culmination of history, God will bring His purposes for Jesus Christ, for mankind in general, and for Israel in particular, to completion during this golden age.

Rightful Rule Restored

Christ's millennial reign will restore the creation to its rightful order that was interrupted and thrown into disarray when sin entered the human race. The most important purpose achieved in the millennium is the fact that Jesus Christ will take His rightful throne as Ruler of the earth. He was ordained by God to rule, and that purpose will be gloriously fulfilled during this time.

Mankind's purpose and divine destiny will also be realized during the millennium. God told Adam and Eve to have dominion over the creation (Gen. 1:26–28; see Psalm 8:6–8), a dominion they forfeited when they sinned.

But then Jesus Christ, the last Adam, replaced the first Adam as head of the human race when He died for sin and rose victoriously over sin and death and Satan. So when Christ rules, we will rule with Him as God reverses the effects of sin and restores to mankind the dominion He commanded the human race to exercise back in Eden.

In fact, the Bible often compares Christ's kingdom to Eden. The prophet Ezekiel wrote, "They will say, 'This desolate land has become like the garden of Eden; and the waste, desolate and ruined cities are fortified and inhabited'" (Ezek. 36:35; see Isa. 51:3).

The first Adam was created in a perfect environment of absolute innocence. But the kingdom will be even better because the last Adam will reign in a perfect environment of absolute righteousness.

Fulfillment for Israel

The millennium will also mean the completion and fulfillment of God's purposes for Israel. God promised concerning Israel, "'I will also plant them on their land, and they will not again be rooted out from their land which I have given them,' says the LORD your God" (Amos 9:15).

God not only promised Israel that He would give them their land, but that they would be permanent residents of *all* the land. That's not the case today. Israel inhabits only a portion of the land God promised to Abraham. But in the millennial kingdom, Israel will get all of its land back.

Israel will also have its rightful King in the millennium. Jesus was rejected when He came the first time to present Himself to the Jews as their King. His birth in Bethlehem fulfilled God's promise of a King, as the religious leaders of Israel acknowledged when the Magi came to them (Matt. 2:6).

But Jesus illustrated Israel's rejection of Him in His parable of the nobleman who went away to receive a kingdom. His subjects sent the nobleman this message: "We do not want this man to reign over us" (Luke 19:14). That was the official position of Israel concerning Jesus. But God had promised David that his Son would rule on his throne forever. Jesus Christ is that Son of David, and He will take the throne in Jerusalem and reign in His kingdom.

By the way, Christ's rule in Jerusalem will be a righteous dictatorship. "It will come about that in the last days the mountain of the house of the LORD will be established as the chief of the mountains, and will be raised above the hills; and all the nations will stream to it" (Isa. 2:2).

Jerusalem will be the capital of the world in the millennium (Isa. 2:3; Jer. 3:17–18; Zech. 14:16), which is why at Armageddon the battle will be for control of Jerusalem. The kingdom will be Israel's golden age of restoration and the realization of all that God promised and purposed for His chosen people.

Revealing the Source of Sin

Here's an interesting fact about the millennium that I want to note before we move on. This period will reveal the true source of the sin that has infected the human race since Adam, and it will also bring an end to sin. We need to recall that during this thousand-year period, even with Satan locked away (Rev. 20:1–3), sin will still be brewing in the hearts of many people.

It's clear that the King will tolerate no rebellion during His reign. Christ will deal with any hint of rebellion swiftly and righteously. But there will be people born in the millennium who do not want Christ to rule over them, and when Satan is released for a short time at the end of the kingdom, these rebels will follow him to destruction.

So how does the millennium reveal the true source of sin? By showing that the real sin problem is in the human heart. There will be no devil—no tempter, no liar, no deceiver—active in the kingdom. No one will be deceived or tempted or tricked by Satan into sin. With Satan bound, we understand that his demons will also be out of commission, so that there will also be no demonically inspired temptation during the millennium.

Therefore, those who choose to reject King Jesus and rebel will do so out of the evil in their own hearts. They will opt for sin even in the midst of a perfect environment with a perfectly righteous Ruler on the throne. The millennium will reveal that the cause of sin is not just the devil or the environment, but the evil in human hearts. And the end of the millennium will bring about the end of sin.

THE CHURCH IN THE MILLENNIUM

Revelation 19:7–9 describes the great event awaiting the church when Christ comes for His bride:

> "Let us rejoice and be glad and give the glory to Him, for the marriage of the Lamb has come and His bride has made herself ready." It was given to her to clothe herself in fine linen, bright and clean; for the fine linen is the righteous acts of the saints.
>
> Then he said to me, "Write, 'Blessed are those who are invited to the marriage supper of the Lamb.'"

The marriage supper of Jesus Christ, at which He will receive His bride, the church for which He died (see Eph. 5:25–27), is going to be a glorious occasion. Every Christian became a part of Christ's bride, the church, and became engaged to Him at the moment of our salvation. We belong to Christ, even though we have not yet come to the wedding ceremony. Therefore, to give ourselves to anyone or anything else is spiritual adultery.

Reigning with Christ

As Christ's bride in the kingdom, we will reign with Him the way a king's wife shares his throne. Paul said the church will judge the world and even angels (see 1 Cor. 6:2–3), and in Revelation 20:4 John said the resurrected saints will reign with Christ for a thousand years.

The Bible says we are "fellow heirs" with Christ (Rom. 8:17), and our level of authority in the kingdom depends on our faithfulness to Him on earth. That explains why in His parable of the servants, Jesus rewarded the first two servants with authority over ten cities and five cities, respectively (Luke 19:15–19). Jesus is going to administer His kingdom through us.

THE CHARACTER OF THE MILLENNIUM

The first thing I want us to see is that during the millennium, mankind will enjoy the long life people have always wished for. Length of life will be immaterial to the believers who are raptured and come back with Christ, because we will have our resurrection bodies. But those who are saved at the end of the tribulation, the ones Jesus calls His sheep (Matt. 25:31–40), will enter the millennium in their natural bodies and procreate, as we have already seen.

They will live on an earth returned to its original perfection and beauty and fruitfulness, an environment in which long life will be the norm: "No longer will there be in it an infant who lives but a few days, or an old man who does not live out his days; for the youth will die at the age of one hundred and the one who does not reach the age of one hundred will be thought accursed" (Isa. 65:20).

A Time of Fulfillment

I love this characteristic about the millennium. All of the limitations and frustrations we experience here on earth will be lifted. Isaiah says:

> They will build houses and inhabit them;
> They will also plant vineyards and eat their fruit.
> They will not build and another inhabit,
> They will not plant and another eat;
> For as the lifetime of a tree, so will be the days of My people. . . .
> They will not labor in vain,
> Or bear children for calamity. (65:21–22a, 23)

Your work won't be in vain in the kingdom. You won't see your best efforts fail or go up in smoke, or build something only to watch someone else take it over. You'll enjoy the fruit of your own work in the kingdom. There will be no unfulfillment.

Let me show you a wonderful passage that captures the character of Jesus Christ's reign. The prophet Isaiah said of the King who will rule, "The Spirit of the LORD will rest on Him" (Isa. 11:2). Isaiah then went on to describe the fullness of the Spirit that will rest on Christ.

Because Christ rules in the fullness of the Holy Spirit, His administration will be totally different than any government we have ever seen. For example:

> And He will delight in the fear of the LORD,
> And He will not judge by what His eyes see,
> Nor make a decision by what His ears hear;

But with righteousness He will judge the poor,
And decide with fairness for the afflicted of the earth;
And He will strike the earth with the rod of His mouth,
And with the breath of His lips He will slay the wicked.
Also righteousness will be the belt about His loins,
And faithfulness the belt about His waist. (vv. 3–5)

People say they want justice and honesty from their rulers. We have a hard time today finding people of integrity who can occupy the offices of government. But that will not be a problem when Jesus Christ takes the reins of government.

His administration in the millennial kingdom will result in a thousand years of perfect justice and righteousness. The earth will also abound with health and prosperity (Isa. 29:18; 32:2–4; 33:24; 35:5–6). All of this will take place because the earth will be filled with the knowledge of God (Isa. 11:9; 32:15; 44:3), and God will personally communicate to the hearts of His people (Jer. 31:33–34).

THE CULMINATION OF THE MILLENNIUM

When the millennium comes to an end and the thousand years are completed, the Bible says that "Satan will be released from his prison" (Rev. 20:7) to gather all the rebels for one more run at overthrowing God.

Satan will "come out to deceive the nations" and will amass an army of rebels so great its number "is like the sand of the seashore" (Rev. 20:8). Satan's army will surround Jerusalem, but this fight will be over before it starts, because "fire came down from heaven and devoured them" (v. 9).

Then the devil will finally and forever get his due. "The devil who deceived them was thrown into the lake of fire and brimstone, where the beast and the false prophet are also; and they will be tormented day and night forever and ever" (v. 10).

We know that there will be people in the millennium who refuse Christ and want to rebel against His rule. But even when we read it in Scripture, it seems hard to believe that people will rebel in a perfect environment.

Even so, out of that mass of humanity, Satan will find enough sinners to gather an army that can't be counted. Yet this brief rebellion will be the final expression of Satan and the final expression of sinful man. History will culminate in Satan's final rebellion and his eternal judgment. Those who belong to Christ will be ushered into eternity, and those who refuse Him will come up before God for the great white throne judgment. History will end with God's final and complete victory.

Handing Over the Kingdom

According to 1 Corinthians 15:24–26, at the end of the millennium Jesus Christ will hand over the reins of authority to God the Father. Paul described this amazing moment:

> Then comes the end, when He hands over the kingdom to the God and Father, when He has abolished all rule and all authority and power. For He must reign until He has put all His enemies under His feet. The last enemy that will be abolished is death.

Christ will defeat all of His enemies in a perfect reign as King, and then deliver His kingdom to the Father to extend the rule of heaven into eternity. What was true of the millennial kingdom will become the normal, eternal operation of heaven. Jesus Christ will turn to His Father and say, "I have fulfilled My reign. The kingdom is Yours."

The church's calling is to set in place the mechanisms of God's kingdom agenda. The reason we study prophecy is not to satisfy our curiosity, but to learn how we are to carry out our lives while we look for our King's return.

12

PROPHECY AND THE GREAT WHITE THRONE

You've probably watched at least one of those episodes of a series that feature amazing or frightening or dramatic events caught on tape. Cameras on phones in today's world make it possible to record almost anyone doing almost anything.

One series of these programs features employees caught doing all kinds of illegal or ridiculous things at work. On one show, a clerk in a department store was filmed taking money from a customer and slipping it into her pocket instead of the cash register. The clerk transferred the money with such a quick and slight move that it would never have been detected, except for the fact that a surveillance camera was in the ceiling directly above her filming the theft.

As the hosts on these shows often say, the camera doesn't blink, and it doesn't lie—even though a lot of "caught on tape" shows are filled with stuff the person on camera didn't want anyone to see.

This is about the closest illustration I can find of what it will be like for the unbelievers who must stand before God in judgment at the end of the millennium. We could also compare it to a medical CAT scan, which looks past a person's outer attire to reveal the true condition of the inner organs.

This judgment is the last event in time before God ushers in eternity, and so in one sense it is the termination point of His prophetic program for mankind. It is best known by the description of the seat upon which the Judge will sit.

John said, "I saw a great white throne" (Rev. 20:11). The white throne judgment is the event most people are referring to when they talk about "judgment day" in terms of having to face God. Let's look at the details of this judgment in which unrepentant sinners "fall into the hands of the living God" (Heb. 10:31).

THE PARTICIPANTS IN THE JUDGMENT

The most important participant in this final judgment of mankind is the Judge Himself—although interestingly enough, He is not identified by name. But this is an awesome person "from whose presence earth and heaven fled away" (Rev. 20:11). That can only be a description of Deity, and so we understand that the Judge is a member of the Godhead.

The Judge is Jesus Himself, who has already been sitting on the throne in Jerusalem ruling and judging the world for one thousand years. Besides, He has just defeated Satan and his rebellious forces at the climax of the millennium (v. 10), so He is already exercising judgment. The whiteness of the throne speaks of Christ's purity and holiness.

We can also be confident this Judge is Jesus Christ because He said, "Not even the Father judges anyone, but He has given all judgment to the Son" (John 5:22; see Acts 17:31). Then in verse 27 of

John 5, Jesus said the Father "gave Him authority to execute judgment, because He is the Son of Man."

Why is Jesus Christ seated on the throne executing God's judgment? Because He is the Son of Man, who paid the price for man's sin and can relate to the people He is judging since He also took on human flesh. Of course, Jesus is also the Son of God, so He can relate to God's justice. He is the perfect Judge to sit on this great white throne.

Who else is present at this judgment? "I saw the dead, the great and the small, standing before the throne. . . . And the sea gave up the dead which were in it, and death and Hades gave up the dead which were in them; and they were judged" (Rev. 20:12–13). The defendants at this judgment are the unbelievers of all the ages, the people whose names are not found in the Book of Life (v. 15). No Christians are anywhere to be found at this judgment. The penalty for their sins has been laid on Christ, and their names written in His Book of Life. At this point, Christians have already been evaluated for their service at the judgment seat of Christ prior to the kingdom.

Notice that those unbelievers who had died before this judgment will be raised from the dead to face their condemnation. This is the "resurrection of judgment" Jesus spoke about (John 5:29). Death is no barrier to God.

The great white throne will be unlike any courtroom we have seen because it will have a Judge but no jury, a prosecutor but no defense attorney, and a sentence but no appeal. None of those things will exist in this courtroom because Christ will judge the unbelieving world with absolute justice. Nothing will be missed or overlooked as unsaved people from throughout history appear before Christ in the final judgment of the ages.

THE PURPOSES OF THE JUDGMENT

What purposes of God will be accomplished when Jesus sits on the great white throne at the end of time? I see at least four things this judgment will do.

To Purge Sin from the Universe

When Christ finishes judging the world from His white throne, the world will be finally and forever purged of the sin that has plagued it since the day Eve was seduced by the tempter.

We have seen that at various points in God's prophetic plan, He will deal with sin and judge sinners. But even during the millennium, sin and rebellion will be brewing in the hearts of multitudes of people. And at the end of this time, Satan will still have one last gasp.

But all sin will be swept into hell forever at God's great white throne judgment. Revelation 21:1 shows that immediately after the final judgment, the new heaven and new earth appear. The order of events is important here because God can't introduce His new creation while sin is still polluting the environment.

John said heaven and earth will flee from Christ's presence when He comes to judge (Rev. 20:11). These are the old heaven and old earth, and they won't come back. They will be replaced by the new ones once sin has been purged from the universe.

To Vindicate God's Perfect Justice

Since God's judgment is never unfair or arbitrary, the sinners who stand before Christ at the great white throne will be judged "according to their deeds" (Rev. 20:12–13). God says it twice to emphasize the justice of this trial.

We often hear it said that people are condemned to hell not because of the terrible things they did, but because they rejected Christ as their Savior and Sin-Bearer. This is true—so why does the Bible say sinners will be judged according to their deeds at the great white throne? The reason is that God will put their ideas of right and wrong up against His holy and perfect standard to show them how far short of His standard they have fallen.

Christians are people who have admitted that they are sinners who can't save themselves, and they have thrown themselves on the mercy and grace of God in Christ. They have accepted Jesus Christ's payment for their sins.

Many unbelievers may agree that they are sinners, but they think they aren't all that bad by their standards. They think their sin isn't that big of a deal, and it will be outweighed by the good things they have done. But at the judgment, their sins will be displayed against the perfect holiness of God, and suddenly it will be a very big deal. Most unbelievers will never understand the holiness and perfect justice of God until they see it at the judgment.

I don't know about you, but when I am dealing with a perfect God, I don't want to be judged according to my deeds. But a lot of unbelievers are like the ruler who came to Jesus and claimed he had kept the Law (Luke 18:18–21). He was willing to be judged by his deeds because he didn't understand that the only standard acceptable to God is absolute perfection. So at the final judgment, sinners will finally see the awfulness of their sin because it will be revealed in the blazing light of God's justice.

Now having said this, let me back up and affirm that the reason people will be sent to hell is their lack of a saving relationship with Christ. Revelation 20:15 says they will be thrown into the lake of fire not because of their deeds, but because they weren't in the Lamb's Book of Life. And the only way you can get your name in this book is by accepting Christ.

To Determine People's Punishment

A third purpose of the white throne judgment is to determine the degree of punishment unbelievers will receive in hell. This aspect of the judgment isn't found explicitly in Revelation 20, although it is suggested by the fact that the books of people's deeds are opened. But there is abundant evidence in Scripture that people will be judged based on the knowledge they had and the opportunities they had or didn't have to repent and receive Christ.

We're not talking about *whether* people are punished, but how severely. Any sin will disqualify a person from heaven. But because God is just, there will be degrees of judgment in hell just as there will be degrees of reward for believers in heaven. Some sinners are more blatant and vile than others.

Jesus once pronounced judgment on the cities "in which most of His miracles were done" (Matt. 11:20). He said:

> "Woe, to you, Chorazin! Woe to you, Bethsaida! For if the miracles had occurred in Tyre and Sidon which occurred in you, they would have repented long ago in sackcloth and ashes. Nevertheless I say to you, it will be more tolerable for Tyre and Sidon in the day of judgment than for you. And you, Capernaum, will not be exalted to heaven, will you? You will descend to Hades; for if the miracles had occurred in Sodom which occurred in you, it would have remained to this day. Nevertheless I say to you that it will be more tolerable for the land of Sodom in the day of judgment, than for you." (vv. 21–24)

We know all about Sodom. Jesus wasn't saying the sins of Sodom weren't terrible. He was saying the people of Sodom didn't get to see what the people of Capernaum saw—and by the way, Capernaum was Jesus' headquarters during His ministry. Jesus said, "From everyone who has been given much, much will be required" (Luke 12:48). Here is clear evidence of degrees of punishment in hell.

Based on this we would have to say that unbelievers here in the West, where there is an incredible amount of Christian teaching and access to the gospel, will have a lot more to answer for at the judgment than people who have never heard the name of Jesus. The amount of light people have will affect their judgment.

On another occasion, Jesus warned His hearers about the scribes of that day, who made a great show of their piety and loved to receive honor, yet inwardly were dishonest people who "devour widows' houses." Notice what Jesus said about them: "These will receive greater condemnation" (Mark 12:38–40).

In other words, not all condemnation is equal. Scribes were experts in the Mosaic Law. They were supposed to know more than the average Israelite. They had greater exposure to God's Word. So they would be judged by a stricter standard.

We see the same principle in the judgment of "the great harlot" (Rev. 19:2), Babylon, that will corrupt the earth during the great tribulation:

> Pay her back even as she has paid, and give back to her double according to her deeds; in the cup which she has mixed, mix twice as much for her. To the degree that she glorified herself and lived sensuously, to the same degree give her torment and mourning. (Rev. 18:6–7)

People often wonder if murderous tyrants like Adolf Hitler and Joseph Stalin will be punished more severely for their horrible sins. I believe the Bible teaches that they will be. We need to distinguish between the effect sin has on our standing before God and the impact of our sin on others.

Satan, the Antichrist, and the False Prophet will receive the most severe punishment because they led so many others astray. That's why the Bible warns that spiritual teachers will be judged by a stricter standard (James 3:1).

All sin is equally sinful to God, and no sinner can stand in His presence. But sins are not all equal in their impact. Stealing a cookie is not as devastating in its effect as murder. God's law allowed differing levels of punishment for differing levels of crimes, and God will apply the same standards at the great white throne.

To Reveal Man's Responsibility

A fourth purpose of this judgment is to show once and for all that people are responsible for their sins. I have already suggested this purpose in our discussion of the books that contain people's deeds. No one will be able to dodge responsibility or blame God for his or her sins, because the records of all deeds will be there in perfect order. Someone might say, "That's not fair. What about all the good deeds these people did?" There are at least two answers to that question.

First, remember that when it comes to God's perfect standard, there *are* no good deeds acceptable to God apart from Christ. The best that people can do on their own is in reality "a filthy garment" in God's sight (Isa. 64:6). So there won't be any good deeds people can present in their defense at the judgment.

Second, even if unbelievers could bring their good deeds to the judgment, these would still be irrelevant to the issue at hand. The only thing that will matter is whether a person's name is in the Book of Life.

Imagine a person who is found guilty of theft. The judge asks the defendant if he has anything to say before sentence is pronounced. The guilty party responds, "Your honor, I have never killed anyone. I have obeyed the traffic laws. I love my children and am devoted to my wife."

The judge will respond, "Those things are nice, but they are irrelevant to this court. You are being sentenced for the theft you committed."

If you ask people why they think they are going to heaven, many will tell you they believe they're going to make it because they are basically good people. They think they have enough goodness stored up to satisfy God.

But standing before Christ at His great white throne, their sin will appear "utterly sinful" (Rom. 7:13) and their supposed goodness will evaporate. People will see God as He is and see their sin for what it really is. And they will know they are responsible for their sins, without any excuse to offer.

THE PATTERN OF THE JUDGMENT

What pattern will Jesus Christ follow in His judgment at the great white throne? What standard will He use in executing judgment? I want to suggest that three books will be present at this tribunal.

The Word of God

Jesus said in John 12:48 that the Word He spoke will be the standard by which those who reject Him will be judged "at the last day." When the ruler came to Jesus seeking eternal life, Jesus cited the Ten Commandments, thereby suggesting that these were the standards by which this man would be judged (Luke 18:20).

The Bible is God's standard of judgment because it is the only revelation of His will and His commands. A person cannot be judged and condemned for breaking a law that doesn't exist. God will judge people by His Word.

Jesus illustrated this principle in the story of the slave who knew his master's will, but "did not get ready or act in accord with his [master's] will" (Luke 12:47). That slave was punished with "many lashes" for failing to obey his master's word even though he knew it. People will be held responsible for the truths found in God's Word. A man once told me he was leaving our church in Dallas because he was learning too much of the Bible, and he didn't want to be held accountable for having greater knowledge. I've heard a lot of excuses in my years of ministry, but that one was unique. This man was trying to run from the Word, but the Bible says, "To one who knows the right thing to do and does not do it, to him it is sin" (James 4:17). God's Word will be the standard of judgment at the great white throne.

The Book of Deeds

We've discussed the contents of this book previously, so I just want to mention the book of deeds as the second volume to be used in the process of final judgment. Ecclesiastes 12:14 says God will bring every act into judgment. The Word of God will pronounce the doom of unbelievers, and being faced with the record of their sins will have the effect of confirming the rightness of God's judgment.

The Book of Life

We have also mentioned the Book of Life, which is sometimes called "the *Lamb's* book of life" (Rev. 21:27, italics added). This is Jesus' book, filled with the names of the people whom He purchased with His precious blood. As we said, none of the people in this book will have to appear at the great white throne. This book is only there to verify the lost condition of those whose names are not in it.

As John was describing the New Jerusalem, he said the only people who will be allowed to enter the Celestial City are those whose names are in the Book of Life (Rev. 21:27). Believers are told to rejoice in their salvation (see Luke 10:20), but the tragedy of the great white throne is that no one there will be found in the book. Those who come to Christ by faith have their names *eternally* recorded in His book (Luke 10:20), where no eraser can ever remove them.

THE PUNISHMENT AT THE JUDGMENT

The punishment Jesus Christ will mete out at the great white throne judgment has a definite sense of finality to it. "Death and Hades were thrown into the lake of fire. This is the second death, the lake of fire. And if anyone's name was not found written in the book of life, he was thrown into the lake of fire" (Rev. 20:14–15).

The Second Death

John said the lake of fire is "the second death." To experience a second death, there must have been a first death. The first death that mankind experienced was original sin, which takes us back all the way to the beginning of time in Eden.

When God commanded Adam not to eat from the Tree of the Knowledge of Good and Evil, He added this warning, "In the day that you eat from it you will surely die" (Gen. 2:17). Adam and Eve ate from the tree and died the same day—not physically, but spiritually. They were driven from the garden and from God's presence and saddled with the curse of sin.

This was the first death. It consisted of lost fellowship with God. When our first parents sinned, the human race was banned from Paradise, cut off from God, and sent out to live in a world cursed by thorns and weeds and sickness and physical death.

In His death on the cross, Jesus Christ provided redemption from the curse of sin by taking the curse on Himself and paying the price for sin (see Gal. 3:13). Therefore, if you are a Christian you are removed from the curse.

In other words, the effects of the first death can be reversed. But the second death is irreversible. It is eternal. Like the first death, the second death involves removal from God's presence, except that this removal is forever. The second death is permanent separation from God's grace and mercy.

The Absence of God's Greatness

Let me make an important theological point here. God is omnipresent. He is everywhere. He fills all of creation. David asked, "Where can I flee from Your presence?" (Ps. 139:7). Answer: nowhere. The presence of God is a reality even in hell. When we say people in hell are eternally separated from God, we are talking about His grace and mercy and salvation. Those who suffer condemnation at the great white throne will find none of these attributes of God in hell. They are unavailable.

This horrific, devastating fact is the real torment of hell. Imagine being in a place totally devoid of God's goodness. Do you realize that *every* good thing we enjoy in life is possible only because God is good (see James 1:17)?

An Eternity of Evil

Here's another terrible aspect of the second death. "Let the one who does wrong, still do wrong; and let the one who is filthy, still be filthy; and let the one who is righteous, still practice righteousness; and the one who is holy, still keep himself holy" (Rev. 22:11). Whatever a person's nature, that person will be locked into it for all eternity.

So a filthy, vile person on earth will exist eternally as a filthy, vile person. There is no moral improvement in hell because hell is not restorative punishment. It will be too late for that. Hell is retributive punishment.

You may wonder why it matters what people will be like in hell. It matters because the Bible is giving us the real deal so no one in his right mind would refuse Christ for eternity in hell. Along with the absence of God's goodness, hell will be torment because sinners will have all of their same evil cravings with no capacity to satisfy them. A sexually immoral person will burn for sex, but there will be none. The jealous person will burn with jealousy, but there will be no way to fulfill those jealous longings. Sinners will be confirmed in their evil character and their lostness.

Unfit for Heaven

Because people who are judged at the great white throne will remain in their sinful condition in hell, they wouldn't be able to enjoy heaven even if God allowed them to enter. Sinners in hell are totally unfit for heaven, in other words.

People in hell wouldn't want to go to heaven even if they could, because they would actually be more miserable in heaven than they are in hell. As horrible as hell will be, it will be preferable to heaven for the condemned.

Now you say, "Tony, how in the world can that be true?" Here's what I mean. We could call the second death the eternal version of the first death since the essence of both is banishment from the merciful and gracious presence of God.

Before Adam and Eve sinned, they had perfect fellowship with God. They were completely at peace in His presence. But the first thing they did after they sinned was hide when they heard God coming (Gen. 3:8).

Adam and Eve chose to run from God because they couldn't bear to be in His presence in their sinful condition. It was too painful, like a person whose eyes are dilated suddenly stepping out into brilliant sunlight. If you have ever been in that condition, you know that darkness is preferable to light because the light is too painful.

That's what would happen if an unredeemed sinner from hell were ever to enter heaven. It wouldn't be relief and joy. It would be incredibly painful, and the sinner would want to run back to the darkness. Hell is the final punishment that will be pronounced on unrepentant sinners at the great white throne judgment.

WHAT BELIEVERS SHOULD DO NOW

Getting a glimpse into what hell will really be like and gaining a greater understanding of prophecy ought to motivate each of us to take part in sharing the gospel of Jesus Christ as much as we can. Whether that means sharing the gospel yourself, or giving to ministries that do, promoting the spread of the gospel should be a focal point of your life goals and daily decisions.

When we had to cancel our tour to Israel due to the war breaking out, and we had to share the disappointing news with the thousand or so attendees who had looked forward to this trip, we were able to give them a refund. This is because going to Israel on the tour was our plan. There was no Plan B for this year. We didn't suggest that they wait a month and let's try again. Nor did we say we could go to another country together. We simply refunded those guests who did not want to wait a few more years until we aim to go again.

When you and I share the gospel with those who are lost, we are sharing the only plan and the only way to heaven. The gospel is the plan. There is no Plan B. There exists no other way to escape God's wrath of hell than to trust in and accept Jesus Christ as Savior. That is how God has set it up to take place. It is my prayer that your study of the Scripture and the subject of prophecy will inspire you to share the gospel with as many people as you can. After all, when it comes to avoiding the horrors of hell, there is no other plan than placing your faith in Jesus.

APPENDIX:
THE URBAN
ALTERNATIVE

The Urban Alternative (TUA) equips, empowers, and unites Christians to impact *individuals, families, churches,* and *communities* through a thoroughly kingdom agenda worldview. In teaching truth, we seek to transform lives.

The core cause of the problems we face in our personal lives, homes, churches, and societies is a spiritual one; therefore, the only way to address it is spiritually. We've tried a political, social, economic, and even a religious agenda.

It's time for a **kingdom agenda**.

The kingdom agenda can be defined as the visible manifestation of the comprehensive rule of God over every area of life.

The unifying central theme throughout the Bible is the glory of God and the advancement of His kingdom. The conjoining thread from Genesis to Revelation—from beginning to end—is focused on one thing: God's glory through advancing God's kingdom.

When you do not recognize that theme, the Bible becomes disconnected stories that are great for inspiration but seem to be unrelated in purpose and direction. Understanding the role of the kingdom in Scripture increases the relevancy of this several thousand-year-old text to your day-to-day living, because the kingdom is not only then; it is now.

The absence of the kingdom's influence in our personal lives, family lives, churches, and communities has led to a deterioration in our world of immense proportions:

- People live segmented, compartmentalized lives because they lack God's kingdom worldview.
- Families disintegrate because they exist for their own satisfaction rather than for the kingdom.
- Churches are limited in the scope of their impact because they fail to comprehend that the goal of the church is not the church itself, but the kingdom.
- Communities have nowhere to turn to find real solutions for real people who have real problems because the church has become divided, ingrown, and unable to transform the cultural and political landscape in any relevant way.

The kingdom agenda offers us a way to see and live life with a solid hope by optimizing the solutions of heaven. When God is no longer the final and authoritative standard under which all else falls, order and hope leaves with Him. But the reverse of that is true as well: as long as you have God, you have hope. If God is still in the picture, and as long as His agenda is still on the table, it's not over.

Even if relationships collapse, God will sustain you. Even if finances dwindle, God will keep you. Even if dreams die, God will revive you. As long as God and His rule are still the overarching standard in your life, family, church, and community, there is always hope.

Our world needs the King's agenda. Our churches need the King's agenda. Our families need the King's agenda.

We've put together a three-part plan to direct us to heal the divisions and strive for unity as we move toward the goal of truly being one nation under God. This three-part plan calls us to assemble with others in unity, address the issues that divide us, and to act together for social impact. Following this plan, we will see individuals, families, churches, and communities transformed as we follow God's kingdom agenda in every area of our lives. You can request this plan by emailing info@tonyevans.org or by going online to tonyevans.org.

In many major cities, there is a loop that drivers can take when they want to get somewhere on the other side of the city but don't necessarily want to head straight through downtown. This loop will take you close enough to the city so that you can see its towering buildings and skyline, but not close enough to actually experience it.

This is precisely what we, as a culture, have done with God. We have put Him on the "loop" of our personal, family, church, and community lives. He's close enough to be at hand should we need Him in an emergency, but far enough away that He can't be the center of who we are.

We want God on the "loop," not the King of the Bible who comes downtown into the very heart of our ways. Leaving God on the "loop" brings about dire consequences as we have seen in our own lives and with others. But when we make God, and His rule, the centerpiece of all we think, do, or say, it is then that we will experience Him in the way He longs for us to experience Him.

He wants us to be kingdom people with kingdom minds set on fulfilling His kingdom's purposes. He wants us to pray, as Jesus did, "Not my will, but Thy will be done." Because His is the kingdom, the power, and the glory.

There is only one God, and we are not Him. As King and Creator, God calls the shots. It is only when we align ourselves underneath His comprehensive hand that we will access His full power and authority in all spheres of life: personal, familial, ecclesiastical, and governmental.

As we learn how to govern ourselves under God, we then transform the institutions of family, church, and society using a biblically based kingdom worldview.

Under Him, we touch heaven and change earth.

To achieve our goal, we use a variety of strategies, approaches, and resources for reaching and equipping as many people as possible.

BROADCAST MEDIA

Millions of individuals experience *The Alternative with Dr. Tony Evans* through the daily radio broadcast playing on nearly **1,400 Radio outlets** and in over **130 countries**. The broadcast can also be seen on several TV networks, and is available online at tonyevans.org. You can also listen or view the daily broadcast by downloading the Tony Evans app for free in the app store. Over thirty million message downloads/streams occur each year.

LEADERSHIP TRAINING

The Tony Evans Training Center (TETC) facilitates a comprehensive discipleship platform which provides an educational program that embodies the ministry philosophy of Dr. Tony Evans as expressed through the kingdom agenda. The training courses focus on leadership development and discipleship in the following five tracks:

- Bible & Theology
- Personal Growth
- Family & Relationships
- Church Health & Leadership Development
- Society & Community Impact Strategies

The TETC program includes courses for both local and online students. Furthermore, TETC programming includes course work for non-student attendees. Pastors, Christian leaders, and Christian laity, both local and at a distance, can seek out The Kingdom Agenda Certificate for personal, spiritual, and professional development. For more information, visit TonyEvansTraining.org.

The Kingdom Agenda Pastors (KAP) provides a *viable network* for *like-minded pastors* who embrace the kingdom agenda philosophy. Pastors have the opportunity to go deeper with Dr. Tony Evans as they are given greater biblical knowledge, practical applications, and resources to impact individuals, families, churches, and communities. KAP welcomes *senior and associate pastors* of all churches. KAP also offers an annual Summit held each year in Dallas with intensive seminars, workshops, and resources. For more information, visit KAFellowship.org.

Pastors' Wives Ministry, founded by the late Dr. Lois Evans, provides *counsel, encouragement,* and *spiritual resources* for pastors' wives as they serve with their husbands in the ministry. A primary focus of the ministry is the KAP Summit that offers senior pastors' wives a safe place to *reflect, renew,* and *relax* along with training in personal development, spiritual growth, and care for their emotional and physical well-being. For more information, visit LoisEvans.org.

KINGDOM COMMUNITY IMPACT

The outreach programs of The Urban Alternative seek to provide positive impact to individuals, churches, families, and communities through a variety of ministries. We see these efforts as necessary to our calling as a ministry and essential to the communities we serve. With training on how to initiate and maintain programs to adopt schools, or provide homeless services, or partner toward unity and justice with the local police precincts, which creates a connection between the police and our community, we, as a ministry, live out God's kingdom agenda according to our *Kingdom Strategy for Community Transformation*.

The Kingdom Strategy for Community Transformation is a three-part plan that equips churches to have a positive impact on their communities for the kingdom of God. It also provides numerous practical suggestions for how this three-part plan can be implemented in your community, and it serves as a blueprint for unifying churches around the common goal of creating a better world for all of us. For more information, visit tonyevans.org and click on the link to access the 3-Point Plan. A course for this strategy is also offered online through the Tony Evans Training Center.

Tony Evans Films ushers in positive life change through compelling video-shorts, animation, and feature-length films. We seek to build kingdom disciples through the power of story. We use a variety of platforms for viewer consumption and have over 120 million digital views. We also merge video-shorts and film with relevant Bible study materials to bring people to the saving knowledge of Jesus Christ and to strengthen the body of Christ worldwide. *Tony Evans Films* released the first feature-length film, *Kingdom Men Rising*, in April 2019 in over eight hundred theaters nationwide, in partnership with Lifeway Films. The second release, *Journey with Jesus*, is in partnership with RightNow Media and was released in theaters in November 2021.

RESOURCE DEVELOPMENT

We are fostering lifelong learning partnerships with the people we serve by providing a variety of published materials. Dr. Evans has published more than 125 unique titles based on over fifty years of preaching whether that is in booklet, book, or Bible study format. He also holds the honor of writing and publishing the first full-Bible commentary and study Bible by an African American, released in 2019. This Bible sits in permanent display as a historic release, in The Museum of the Bible in Washington, DC.

For more information, and a complimentary copy of Dr. Evans's devotional newsletter, call (800) 800–3222 *or* write TUA at P.O. Box 4000, Dallas TX 75208, *or* visit us online.

tonyevans.org

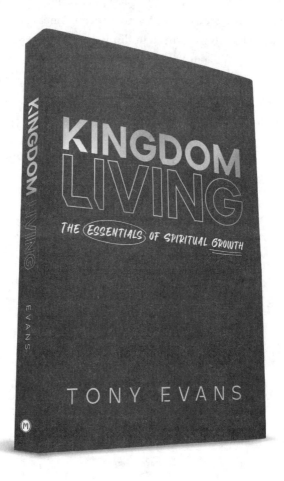

ONENESS IS HARD TO ACHIEVE. LET THE KINGDOM UNITY OF SCRIPTURE POINT THE WAY.

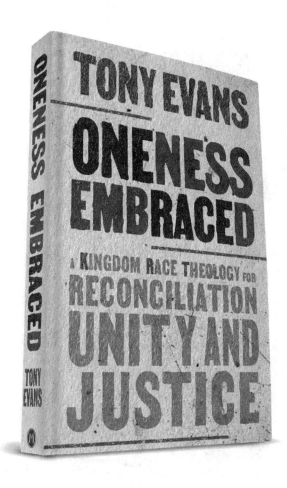

GOD'S KINGDOM ISN'T JUST ABOUT THEOLOGY AND CHURCH.

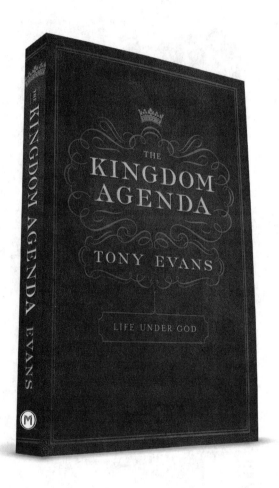

MOODY Publishers

From the Word to Life

God's kingdom isn't just about theology and church. It is about a whole new way of seeing the world and your place in it. *The Kingdom Agenda* offers a fresh and powerful vision that will help you think differently about your life, your relationships, and your walk with God.

Also available as an eBook